Discoveri

New Information on How to Give Your Canine Pal
a Longer, Healthier Life
(And who doesn't want that?)

By Chris Zink DVM PhD DACVSMR

Canine Sports Productions
www.caninesports.com

Discovering Your Dog

New Information on How to Give Your Canine Pal a Longer, Healthier Life

Copyright © 2022 Chris Zink

All rights reserved. No part of this book may be used or reproduced in any form or by any means electronic or mechanical, including photocopying, recording or by any information storage or retrieval system without the prior written permission of the publisher.

For information contact:
Canine Sports Productions, Inc.
info@caninesports.com
www.CanineSports.com

Cover photo by Patrycja Kwiatkowska

All service marks, trademarks, and product names used in this publication belong to their respective holders.

First Edition
First Printing 2022
ISBN 978-1-888119-10-7

To my lifetime's worth of amazing canine teachers: Lucky, Pepi, Beau, Shauna, Shane, Cajun, Bannor, Tally, Stripe, Otter, Fate, Vespa, Hobby, and Helix. Thank you for so patiently sharing life's greatest lessons with me.

Acknowledgements

So many people to thank, so little time. At the top of my list are Gayle Watkins PhD, Donna Raditic DVM DACVIM (Nutrition), and Samra Elser DVM PhD, who gave of their limited free time to read and contribute to many of these chapters during their inception. The advice they provided, based on their deep experience and knowledge of dogs, has made this book much richer than if it all just came out of my head. Thank you also to Robin Sundstrom, whose exquisite knowledge of English grammar made this book much more professional than it otherwise would have been.

This book would still be sitting in pieces on my desk if it were not for Nicole Barrett and Amy Rutter-Hanzel, my assistants who are always there, on a moment's notice, to fix something, find something, or pick up the parts of a project that is half-complete and needs their talented hands.

I have been so lucky to be mentored in all things dog by other dog afficionados, each one generously enlightening me in their own way. You have broadened my knowledge beyond what a lifetime full of dogs could have provided. My thanks go to the late Rachel Page Elliott, and to Sue Sternberg, Cynthia Fox, Marcia Halliday, Marcia Schlehr, Gayle Watkins, Julie Daniels, Magda Chiarella, Carl DeStefano, Donna Brown, Cynthia Hornor, Laurene Galgano, and Ernesto Lara. To any others that I might have failed to mention – my sincerest apologies.

To my veterinary colleagues who have shared their knowledge of the art and science of medicine and who have laughed and cried with me over canine patients: Drs. Marian Shaw, Rosemary LoGiudice, Noel Fitzpatrick, Ryan Gallagher, Janet Van Dyke, Peter Lotsikas, Faith Lotsikas, Pedro Rivera, Sherman Canapp, and Debra Canapp.

Finally, to those who have attended my lectures and seminars, read my books, and watched my videos over the past decades. I am grateful for the many lessons you have taught me.

Contents

Table of Contents
Why your dog wants you to read this book

Fitness & Health
1. Increase Your Dog's Health & Longevity   2
2. Evaluating Your Dog's Fitness   3
3. Be Strong!   5
4. Begging for Answers   8
5. Is Your Dog Hardcore?   11
6. Let's Not (Static) Stretch the Truth   16
7. Proprioception   20
8. Overloaded   25
9. Build Stamina, Prevent Injuries   28
10. Reducing Injury Risk: The Facts!   32
11. Stop Taking Your Dog For Walks!   34
12. Play Ball…Safely!   38
13. No Hot Dogs Please!   43
14. Star Light, Star Bright   46
15. Do the Dewclaws?   51
16. Digit Injuries   55
17. A-Frame-Induced Carpal Injuries?   57
18. It's a Real Pain   59
19. My Dog in Rehab Needs Stuff To Do!   62
20. The Genetics of Athletic Success   69
21. Telomeres and Your Dog's Lifespan   71
22. No Weigh!   74
23. How to Make Your Dog Live Longer   76
24. Inflammatory Food   79
25. Smart Supplementation   84
26. Yeast – Yuck!   87
27. The Cure in Curcumin   90

Behavior & Training
28. To Harness or Not to Harness?   94
29. Love, Actually   98
30. How to Make Your Dog More Optimistic   100
31. Scents of Success   103
32. Cold Nose, Warm Sense   106
33. Paw Preference & Dog Emotions   109
34. The Eyes Have It   112
35. Be-Yawn Compare   115
36. Teacher's Pet   117
37. Perfect Practice Doesn't Make Perfect   120
38. Is Your Dog a Social Butterfly?   123
39. Who Is That Dog in the Mirror?   1326
40. Can We Talk About the Ideal Family Dog?   129
41. The Gift of Being the Only Dog   131
Notes   134
Index   148

Why your dog wants you to read this book

For over 40 years I've enjoyed coaching dog lovers, trainers, veterinarians, and other dog professionals via seminars, consultations, books, and other media. I am passionately interested in all things dog, and I love to share my discoveries with others.

This is a collection of some of my recent discoveries about our best friends. Scientists are publishing more information about dog behavior, cognition, and biology than ever before. It's as if they have finally realized how complex and interesting dogs are! In this book I share the results of some of their most fascinating studies, as well as the tips and tricks that dogs and their people have taught me throughout my life.

In these pages, you'll find new and sometimes surprising information to enhance the lives of every dog with which you share your life. Knowledge is a powerful way to strengthen our relationships with these incredible creatures that, in turn, teach us so much about life and love. Here I have provided you with fascinating, fun to read, scientifically based information to help your dog live a long, healthy and active life. What could be better?

--- Chris Zink

Fitness & Health

1. Increase Your Dog's Health & Longevity

Everyone wants to live longer, right? With the Baby Boomer generation entering its 60s and 70s, there has been abundant new research on how to increase longevity. The result? It is impossible to ignore the evidence: **exercise and longevity go hand-in-hand**. And that's true for dogs too.

Here is some of the evidence:
- **Long-term exercise** promotes the continued innervation of muscle fibers, which **delays aging**.
- Individuals who lead active lives have muscle characteristics that are more similar to adults **30 years younger** than to their more sedentary peers.
- **Life-long maintenance of lean body mass** is a **key factor in achieving a long lifespan**.
- Regular **exercise slows and even reverses** the development of the **muscle atrophy** that so often occurs with aging.
- Regular **exercise increases the replication of neurons** in the hippocampus, the part of the brain that is **responsible for memory and learning**.

Given this overwhelming evidence, we owe it to our dogs (and therefore to ourselves) to incorporate fitness exercises into our dog's lives. This is true regardless of the size or age of the dog or whether the dog participates in performance sports or is simply a treasured family member.

An appropriate exercise program incorporates strength, aerobic, proprioceptive (body awareness), and flexibility exercises that are targeted specifically to the needs of the individual dog.

Training and competing in sports alone does not accomplish this – only an individualized program does.

There's an abundance of information on fitness and conditioning throughout this book. In addition, check out www.ForActiveDogs.com for additional information and studies on canine fitness. Let's keep our canine family members happy and active until the very day they leave for the rainbow bridge.

For references, see Notes, p. 134.

2. Evaluating Your Dog's Fitness
Track Your Dog's Fitness to Detect Early Injuries

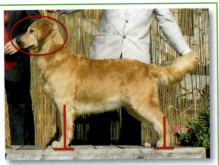

Figure 1. The correct position for assessing muscle size and tone.

Regular assessment of your dog's muscle size and tone should be a **routine part of your dog's health care program**. It will help you **target your dog's conditioning program** to the muscles that most need work and can **tip you off to a possible early injury**.

Set your dog up so that it is standing in a stacked position, just as you would if you were in a conformation show. Here's how to do that (Figure 1):

- Hold each of your dog's **front legs** by the elbow and place your dog's feet so that the radius and ulna are perpendicular to the ground.
- Hold each of your dog's **hocks** (tarsi) and place the rear feet so that the rear pasterns (the part between the hock and the foot) are perpendicular to the ground.
- Hold your dog's **head** up and looking forward with the muzzle parallel to the ground

Once your dog is stacked, assess the **six large muscle groups shown in Figure 2**. It's not necessary to learn the names of the individual muscles. The most important thing is that you know where they are on your dog's body and what they should feel like in a very fit dog.

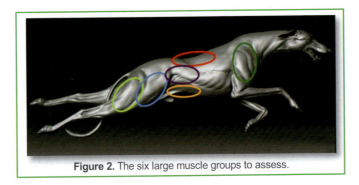

Figure 2. The six large muscle groups to assess.

Starting at the front of the dog, in dark green are the **muscles of the shoulder**, including the supraspinatus, infraspinatus and triceps muscles. Ideally those big muscle bellies should bulge out from the dog's side and should feel firm to the touch.

The next three groups of muscles comprise your dog's **core**, including the paraspinal muscles and the lateral and ventral abdominal muscles. The **paraspinal muscles**, shown in red in Figure 2, are present on both sides of the dorsal spinous processes of the vertebrae, those bony bumps along the center of the back. The tops of these muscles should be as high as the dorsal spinous processes and they should feel very firm to the touch, not soft.

The next two components of the core are the **lateral abdominal muscles** shown in purple on the side of the dog's abdomen in Figure 2, and the **ventral abdominal muscles**, shown in orange. Unlike the other muscles we are checking for fitness, the lateral and ventral abdominal muscles don't get larger - they just get firmer. They often don't feel as firm as the other muscles we're evaluating but they should not feel soft or flabby.

The two groups of rear leg muscles are the **quads**, shown in blue, and the **hamstrings**, in light green. These muscle bellies should feel large and rounded and very firm to the touch. The hamstrings should be larger than the quads, and you should be able to feel the bulging of separate muscle bellies in this group.

> If you've been feeling your dog's muscles as you read along, you probably have a big question mark above your head right now! How are you supposed to know whether the muscles are large or firm enough? Don't worry! That's just because you have nothing with which to compare your dog yet. So go ahead and **assess the muscle size and tone of as many dogs as you can**. Feel your other dogs, feel your friends' dogs. Heck, feel dogs you meet on the street (with their peoples' permission of course)! You will notice huge differences in the firmness of different dogs' muscles and can make it a goal for your own dogs to have the largest, firmest muscles in town! But remember, you must have the dog stacked when doing your assessment.
>
> **SPOTLIGHT**

Figure 3. Check out the incredible muscles on this dog!

QUICK TIP:
Most dogs, as with humans, have weak core muscles. So, if you're having trouble knowing whether your dog's core muscles are strong enough, it's safe to assume that they aren't.

Discovering the Dog
Evaluating Your Dog's Fitness

3. Be Strong!

Many people think that the best way to exercise their dogs is to take them for a walk. Going for a walk on leash is an excellent Good for the Soul exercise, providing sensory stimulation – sights, smells, sounds, new surfaces to walk on, and even some tasty treats (either served by you or discovered in the environment). But **walks do not provide your dog with a balanced exercise program**. Even if you also train your dog for one or more sports and play some fun games like retrieving, your dog still does not experience all the components of a balanced exercise program.

A **balanced exercise program** should contain the following five types of exercises:
- Strength
- Aerobic (cardiopulmonary)
- Proprioception (body awareness)
- Balance
- Flexibility

In this chapter, we'll discuss **strength, which is arguably the most important component of fitness and injury prevention** for active dogs.

Every Dog Needs Strength
A **typical strength exercise for humans is weight-lifting**. Since dogs don't have opposable thumbs, they tend to drop barbells, so for canine strength exercises we use the dog's body as the weight. **Strength exercises are those that require the dog to move its body over short distances**, accelerating, decelerating, turning, etc.

It is easy to incorporate strength training exercises into your dog's life. They are very motivational to your dog because, of course, they involve **food or toy rewards** – lots of them! But there are **three important features** that must be a part of any canine strength-building (resistance) exercise program:

1. Strength exercises should be minimally concussive (low-impact). Active dogs are already experiencing a lot of concussion in training, competition, and just playing – why add more impact on the joints and soft tissues if it isn't necessary? Luckily, there

QUICK TIP:
You can easily incorporate strength exercises into your dog's life with tons of fun and stimulation, in only 10 to 20 minutes three times a week.

Discovering the Dog
Be Strong!

are numerous exercises that are excellent for building a dog's muscular strength without increasing the amount of impact on the body. You can find examples of non-impact strength exercises in Chapters 4, 5, and 19 of this book. In addition, videos of over 25 carefully designed, low-impact strength exercises are available.*

2. Strength exercises should be targeted to the areas of the dog's body that are most in need. To accomplish that, first assess the size and tone of your dog's muscles – the shoulder, back, and abdominal muscles as well as the quads and hamstrings (see Chapter 2). Are they large? If so, that is an indication of long-term exercise, and probably also genetics. Are they firm and well-defined? If so, that is an indication of recent exercise. If not, then that's an area to target when you select your dog's strength exercises.

3. You must overload the muscles to build them. This doesn't mean that your dog should exercise until exhausted. Instead, assess your dog before the exercise – your dog should be ready to work and be warmed up enough so that it is open-mouthed breathing. Stop the exercise when your dog is finding the exercise too difficult to perform correctly. See Chapter 8 for more details.

> **QUICK TIP:**
> The goal of a strength exercise is not to be successful in performing it. In fact, you want your dog to fail. Work your dog a little bit harder each time the exercise is performed – just hard enough that each session brings a significant challenge.

SPOTLIGHT

This dog is demonstrating the Diagonal Leg Lifts exercise to strengthen the core musculature. Diagonally opposite front and rear legs are lifted, and the dog uses its core muscles to help it balance and remain standing.

*A flash drive with dozens of videos demonstrating strength, flexibility, balance, proprioception, and many more exercises can be purchased here: https://caninesports.com/product/ffl-videos/ or videos can be live streamed individually here: https://vimeo.com/ondemand/caninefitforlife

Strength and Speed
Strength is directly related to speed. Picture the bodies of the fastest runners – those that specialize in the 100-m races. Compare their bodies to those of marathon runners, who run at less than half the speed of 100-m runners. Which ones are more muscled?

If you want your dog to be fast at any sport or working job (agility, flyball, obedience, rally, hunt tests, field trials, lure coursing, herding, fast CAT, barn hunts, nosework/scent work, IGP, police/military work, assistance dog work, and search and rescue all require speed or force), **your dog needs to be strong**.

The table below provides **examples of the types of strength activities that our dogs require** to safely and effectively play various sports, perform specific jobs, and just play fun dog games. These examples reveal just how important strength is for active dogs.

Canine Strength Components and Related Activities

Strength	Activity
Acceleration, deceleration, turning, stopping	Most canine sports, working dog jobs, and dog games
Jumping	Agility, flyball, obedience, rally, IGP (IPO/Schutzhund), other protection sports, police/military work, SAR
Driving through vegetation, muddy water, and other environmental obstacles	Hunt tests, field trials, retrieving games
Pulling against a harness	Tracking, mushing, police/military work, SAR, assistance dog work
Lying down and getting up repeatedly	Herding, police/military work, assistance dog work
Heads-up heeling	Obedience, rally, IGP, other protection sports
Bite work	IGP, police/military work, tugging games

Strength Is Associated with Longevity
Regardless age or stage of life, **strength is the most important component** of your dog's exercise program. Active adult dogs that are strong can **reduce their risk of injuries by 66%**. Strength training can even **increase the longevity of senior and geriatric dogs.** Sadly, many senior or geriatric dogs are euthanized every year because they can no longer climb stairs, retain their balance on slippery floors, or sometimes even stand up from a down position. For most of these dogs, **additional core and rear leg strength would allow them to retain their quality of life for months or even years longer.**

Make a Plan
Knowing that strength is so important to your dog, it is important to incorporate exercises that specifically **target your individual dog's areas of weakness**. For example, **many dogs have weak core muscles**; a strength-training program for these dogs should include exercises to specifically work the paraspinal muscles (the back muscles on either side of the vertebrae) and the lateral and ventral abdominal musculature. To know what areas of your dog to target, **regularly and objectively assess your dog's fitness** as described in Chapter 2.

For references, see Notes, p. 134.

4. Begging for Answers?
Try This!

Teaching a dog to **sit up** on its haunches, or **beg**, is **one of the best exercises to strengthen the core musculature –** the paraspinal (back) muscles as well as the lateral and ventral abdominal muscles. This exercise and its variations target all those muscles and can really pay off in preventing injuries in active dogs!

In addition to **targeting specific core muscle groups**, the sit-up **requires no equipment** (except delicious treats), **can be performed indoors** when the weather outside is nasty, and it's **non-concussive**, so you are not adding more impact to your dog's already active life. It checks all the boxes!

But wait a minute! Maybe you have heard that this exercise was not safe for dogs. Some people think that you should never do this exercise with dogs because it would put too much pressure on the articular facets (the joints that connect one vertebra to the next)!

When I heard that rumor, I did what everyone should do, and looked for **scientific evidence**. I went to the best source of published scientific information, scholar.google.com. There I found a study that measured the amount of pressure on dogs' articular facets when they are doing the beg and other exercises. How cool is that? And guess what? **A dog puts MUCH more pressure on its articular facets by just going up or down stairs or transitioning from a sit to a stand than when sitting up in the beg position** (see table below). For me, this puts to rest any concerns about this exercise being dangerous. And this holds for long-bodied dogs like Dachshunds, too. They need core strength even more to support their movements.

Of course, this exercise should not be performed with a dog that has back pain – those dogs need a diagnosis to determine the cause of the pain, which would then be addressed. In addition, this exercise should not be done with a dog that has an iliopsoas strain (stretching or tearing of a muscle that flexes the hip) as it would likely be painful.

Pressures Exerted During Various Exercises

Static Tests		Dynamic (Moving) Tests	
Position	Load Range (N)	Position	Load Range (N)
Sitting	10-65	Climbing stairs	105-170
Standing	60-185	Descending stairs	100-120
Sitting up	15-80	Sit to stand	65-110

So, if any of you were worried that the beg (sit-up) exercise was dangerous, **welcome to one of the best-ever core exercises**!

How To Teach Your Dog to Beg (Sit Up)
Complete this exercise step-by-step – do NOT skip ahead. The goal is not to get to the last stage, but rather to work your dog to overload at each stage before moving to the next. That's the way to build your dog's core strength gradually and safely.

Note: **Always have your dog nibbling on the food** while you are teaching and performing this exercise. This will allow you to off-balance the dog to increase the difficulty of the exercise. And, of course, it increases your dog's love of the game.

Step 1. Getting Your Dog Into the Beg Position
Start with your dog sitting and nibbling the food. Move the food backward and just a little bit upward to a position where it is over the base of your dog's tail, with your dog still nibbling (Figure 1).

Common Training Problems:
If your dog moves away or tries to stand up, first be sure that you are holding the food in a position where your dog can nibble on it continuously. Don't hold the food so high that your dog must stretch its neck up or try to stand up to reach the food. If your dog persists in trying to stand or back up, just put the food behind your back and look away. After a moment, try again. Your dog will quickly realize that they don't get a reward unless they move in the direction in which they were being lured.

Some dogs are initially unable to get their front feet off the ground at all, or perhaps only for a split second. This is usually because their core muscles are weak. If this is the case, give your dog a treat just for trying, even if they lift just one foot slightly off the ground. Try again every couple of days. After eight to 10 days, your dog will have built up enough muscle to be able to beg with both front feet off the ground.

Next, work at getting your dog to balance in the sit-up position for three 15-second reps, with a five-second rest between reps. Only progress to Step 2 when your dog can accomplish this.

Don't give up. I have never met a healthy dog that couldn't do this exercise, given a few days of practice.

Figure 1. With the dog nibbling on food, move the food up and back to get your dog into position.

Step 2. Perturbing Your Dog's Balance

Try to **lure your dog off balance** by moving the food from side to side, backward and forward, up and down. Next, push on your dog's chest or neck from the sides, front and back, at first with a regular rhythm, then irregularly. Try having your dog wave one paw then the other, then both. Use distractors such as dropping food or a ball, tapping your dog's front foot, or other movements to try to trick your dog into moving from the sit-up position. Do not progress to the next level of difficulty until your dog can do three 15-second reps in a row with five seconds of rest in between, with you working to off-balance the entire time.

Step 3. Progressing Through Various Surfaces

Progress through the following surfaces, making sure that your dog can do three 15-second reps on each surface before moving on.
- *Solid, non-slip surface* – this is where you started
- *Level, soft surface* (bed, couch, folded stack of blankets, air mattress). Do not use a disc – the surface should be level.
- *Hills*. Face a different direction each time you train. Gradually increase the incline. The core muscles that are facing uphill do the most work.
- *Egg-shaped physioball*. Place one pointed end against a wall and the other between your knees so that you can move the ball irregularly from side to side.

At each new surface, work to off-balance your dog as described in Step 2 before moving to the next surface. Always ask for three 15-second reps, with five seconds of rest in between before progressing to the next level of difficulty.

QUICK TIP:
Fill the egg-shaped ball so that it is a little soft. Your dog's feet should sink into the surface a few inches when sitting on the ball.

For references, see Notes, p. 135.

5. Is Your Dog Hardcore?

As a veterinarian who is intensely interested in preventing injuries in dogs, I did a study of over 400 dogs that were assessed for front limb, rear limb, and core muscle strength with the goal of determining dogs' weakest areas to target via specific exercises. The data from these dogs showed that **62% of the dogs had weak core muscles,** far more than any other part of the body.

Perhaps you are thinking, "But I have an active performance dog! My dog shouldn't have weak core muscles."

Think again! I was asked to **assess the muscular fitness of 20 of Switzerland's top agility dogs**, many of which were world-class competitors. Any guesses as to **how many of those had strong core muscles**? The answer, stunningly, was exactly **two**!

Dogs can appear perfectly healthy and even compete successfully in high level sports with less than adequate core strength. So, what's the big deal? The answer is, in a word, **injuries**.

Core Muscles have Two Important Jobs
1. They **stabilize** the body by helping the dog hold its posture (such as a level topline) and absorbing sudden forces that could cause injuries (Figure 1).

2. They **mobilize** the body by contributing to rapid movement, force, and power (Figure 1). They create dorsal, ventral, and lateral flexion as well as rotational movements of the body, and they coordinate all movements between the front and rear limbs.

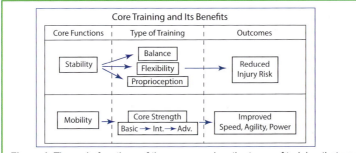

Figure 1. The main functions of the core muscles, the types of training that can be used to strengthen these muscles, and the outcomes of such training.

Weak Core Muscles Increase the Risk of:

a. Back pain/injuries. A weak core may cause the spine to repeatedly hyperextend when your dog is jumping, leaping off a dock or pool edge, or even just running full-out, eventually resulting in **lumbosacral disease.** This condition often requires expensive therapy or even surgery to provide relief from chronic neurological pain.

b. Iliopsoas injuries. With a weak core, your dog has less control over its rear legs, increasing the risk of chronic **iliopsoas strain**, a painful and difficult-to-resolve injury.

c. Cranial cruciate ligament (CCL) injuries. A weak core can prevent your dog from stabilizing its rear legs sufficiently when jumping or turning at speed, eventually resulting in a partial tear or complete rupture of the cranial cruciate ligament. This requires expensive surgery and rehabilitation therapy to reduce the lifetime risk of painful arthritis.

d. Shoulder injuries. If your dog's core is weak, its ability to coordinate and stabilize the front limbs might be impaired enough that the soft tissues that support the shoulder joint can stretch and tear. Damage to these structures results in **supraspinatus tendinopathy**, **biceps tendinopathy,** and/or **medial shoulder syndrome,** requiring expensive corrective surgery followed by months of rehabilitation therapy.

Perhaps you or someone you know have experienced the heartache and hassles that accompany these injuries. Might they have been the result of a weak core? None of us want our dogs to experience these injuries. Nor do we want the expense and lost time of treating them. Luckily, **there are actions you can take now to build your dog's core to help prevent these injuries**.

First, check out Figure 2 to learn about the exact muscles we are talking about, so you can have a better idea of how to improve their function.

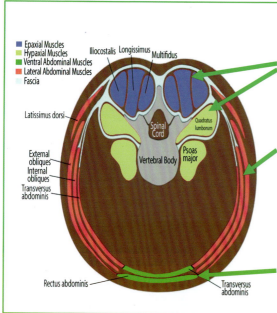

Figure 2. Cross-section through a dog's abdomen. The core muscles form a box. Along the top of the box are the paraspinal muscles (blue and yellow), which surround and support the vertebral bones.

The sides of the box consist of layers of lateral abdominal muscles (red). They support the abdominal organs, stabilize the abdomen against abnormal forces, and help with sideways motions, such as when your dog spins to chase that squirrel that had the audacity to enter your yard.

The bottom of the abdominal box has just two muscles (green), the strongest of which is the *rectus abdominis* – the same one that is responsible for six-pack abs in humans.

How to Strengthen Your Dog's Core Muscles

Since we know that the core muscles form a box around the abdominal organs, it makes sense that movements that flex and extend any of the four sides of the box will strengthen those muscles, right? That's generally true, but there's more to it than that.

As a strong proponent and designer of individualized fitness programs for dogs, I start designing an exercise program by asking some questions about the dog.

1. What is the dog's age?
a. Puppies under six months of age. I don't recommend exercises to strengthen the core muscles in young puppies because their bodies aren't mature enough to deal with those forces yet.

b. Seven months to adult to senior dogs. Dogs in their most active years need BOTH core stability exercises and core mobility exercises.

c. Senior or geriatric dogs. Most older dogs have weak core muscles. Signs include a dipped topline, slow or uncoordinated transitions between sitting, standing, and lying down, and scuffling the rear feet. If your dog shows any of these signs, core exercises are encouraged, but work them gently and progress slowly so as not to cause an injury.

2. What is the dog's current level of core strength?
Where you begin in strengthening your dog's core should be based on its current core strength. You can easily test this by have your dog sit up and beg on its haunches. Don't worry, scientific studies have proven that this is NOT injurious to dogs (see Chapter 4). In fact, **young puppies sit up this way to nurse** (Figure 3)!

If your dog can sit up on its haunches for 15 seconds, you can start with the intermediate core strength exercises described on the next page. If not, start with the basic ones, just to be safe.

Figure 3. Puppies sitting on their haunches to nurse.

Two Types of Core Exercises
1. Core Stability Exercises
All dogs need core stability exercises. Puppies under six months of age and weak senior and geriatric dogs should first pursue core stability exercises before moving to core mobility exercises. Examples of core stability exercises include:
- *Proprioceptive* (body awareness) exercises such as walking SLOWLY forward and backward over the rungs of a ladder placed on the ground (see Chapter 7)
- *Balance* exercises, such as walking and turning along a slightly elevated plank
- *Flexibility* exercises such as play bows and side bending while nibbling on a cookie placed next to the hip or a rear foot (see Chapter 6)

2. Core Mobility Exercises
Core mobility or strength exercises build the dog's paraspinal, lateral abdominal, and ventral abdominal muscles, either individually or together. Ensure that your dog's regular fitness routine focuses on these exercises.

Basic Core Mobility Exercise Examples*
- *Sit-Stand-Sit.* Teach your dog to move between the sit and stand positions with the front feet slightly evaluated and remaining stationary. Gradually elevate the front feet more to make the exercise more difficult.
- *Stand-Down-Stand.* Teach your dog to move between the stand and down positions without moving any feet. Do it on hills, facing different directions to increase difficulty.
- *Roll Over.* Have your dog lie down, roll onto its back and continue all the way back to the down position, all in one continuous motion, three times in a row. Roll in both directions. Roll up hill to increase the difficulty.

Intermediate Core Mobility Exercise Examples*
- *Rocket Dog.* Have your dog sit up and remained balanced on its haunches while nibbling on food (see Chapter 4).

- *Diagonal Leg Lifts.* Lift and hold one front and one rear leg for 30 seconds while your dog uses its core muscles to balance on the other two legs. Stop when your dog fidgets too much or tries to sit down. Once your dog can do three 30-sec lifts alternating each pair of legs, make it harder by standing on uneven or unstable surfaces or hills of gradually increasing inclines.
- *One-Sided Leg Lifts.* Lift and hold one front and one rear leg on the same side of the body for 30 seconds while your dog uses its core muscles to balance on the other two legs. Progress as for diagonal leg lifts.

*A flash drive with videos demonstrating these exercises and many more can be purchased here: https://caninesports.com/product/ffl-videos/ or videos can be live streamed individually here: https://vimeo.com/ondemand/caninefitforlife

Advanced Core Exercise Examples*

- **The Crawl.** Have your dog belly crawl under a coffee table or some bars set at about four to six inches above your dog's back when it is lying in the sphynx position (Figure 4). Your dog should eventually move continuously without stopping to rest its chest on the ground. Make the exercise more difficult by having your dog circle 180 degrees and 360 degrees and crawl backwards.

Figure 4. Alba learning to crawl under chairs.

- **Walking a Peanut Ball.** Have your dog stand on its hind legs while rolling a peanut-shaped exercise ball towards you with its front feet on the ball (Figure 5). Increase the difficulty by having your dog stop, start, change speeds, and roll the ball backwards.

- **Advanced Rocket Dog.** With your dog in the sit-up position and nibbling the food, move the food in all directions so that your dog's head follows the food. Push on your dog in different directions to increase the work they must do to stay balanced. When they are excellent at staying balanced, do the exercise on a level, soft surface such as a bed or couch, then on hills, then on an egg-shaped physioball.

Figure 5. Alba walking a peanut ball forward.

*A flash drive with dozens of videos demonstrating strength, flexibility, balance, proprioception, and many more exercises can be purchased here: https://caninesports.com/product/ffl-videos/ or videos can be live streamed individually here: https://vimeo.com/ondemand/caninefitforlife

For references, see Notes, p. 135.

6. Let's Not (Static) Stretch...
The Truth

Recently I watched a YouTube video of Usain Bolt, the fastest man in the world, performing a warm-up routine. A trainer took each of his legs and put the hip and knee joints into flexion for about one second.

Usain Bolt then did some dynamic stretching, including normal running and running with high knees for short distances, and some sudden accelerations from a stopped position.

A little walking around, and he was ready to go! In the comments section were many submissions such as, "I thought we weren't supposed to stretch!" and "But he's only stretching for a few seconds!" and so on.

Whether or not to stretch, and if so, how and for how long, is a huge controversy in human sports medicine. Since **there are no published articles on the effects of either static or dynamic stretching in dogs**, we must rely on the literature about stretching in humans and apply those findings to dogs. As a result, the same controversy exists in the dog world.

There are numerous articles that say that stretching helps improve human athletic performance. And there are just many that say it doesn't and might even reduce performance. There are numerous articles that say that stretching helps prevent injuries. And there are just as many that say it doesn't. You can see why the subject is so contentious.

As for dogs, they often stretch themselves when they awaken, usually with a nice, long play-bow, and sometimes with an added big rear limb stretch, so it must be helpful, right? I wish it were that easy...

> *Whether or not to stretch, and if so, how and for how long, is a huge controversy in human and canine sports medicine.*

Luckily, there are **two published meta-analyses that have addressed the effects of stretching in human athletes**. A meta-analysis is a statistical analysis that combines the results of multiple scientific studies that address the same question in an attempt to use pooled data to establish a consensus. It is considered the highest form of scientific evidence. The two meta-analyses come to the same conclusions, so we'll just discuss the more recent one.

A meta-analysis examined 125 published studies to determine whether and how **static and dynamic stretching** affected **performance and injury prevention** in sports activities that took place shortly thereafter.

They examined the two main types of stretches: static and dynamic. **Static**, or *passive*, stretching "involves lengthening a muscle until either a stretch sensation or the point of discomfort is felt." It does not involve contraction of muscles, but rather a passive lengthening of the muscle/tendon unit. A canine example of static stretching is shown in Figure 1. Since we are completely unable to discern when our dogs are feeling a "stretch sensation," and given the fact that most dogs hide pain until it is severe, we cannot determine when our dog has reached "the point of discomfort." Therefore, **static stretching as part of a warm-up is inappropriate for dogs**.

Dynamic, or *active*, stretching "involves the performance of a controlled movement through the range of motion of a joint." In dynamic stretching, nerve conduction and muscle contraction occur, so energy-producing mechanisms are activated in the muscle cells, vessels dilate to supply more blood to the muscle, and as a result the muscle heats up. See Figure 2 for an example.

Figure 1. Static (passive) stretching a front leg.

Figure 2. Dynamic (active) stretching the spine.

Results of the Meta-Analysis
1. Static Stretching Effects on Performance
Static stretching **reduced performance** overall by 3.7%. It caused a 1.3% reduction in power-speed-based tasks such as sprinting and jumping, and a 4.8% reduction in strength-based tasks such as maximal voluntary contractions (e.g., how many times a person could perform a task before experiencing overload). **The longer the period of static stretching, the greater the reduction in performance.**

2. Static Stretching Effects on Injury Risk
Only 12 of the 125 studies examined this question, and those covered a wide variety of types and duration of stretches and performance activities. Overall, these studies suggested a **54% risk reduction in acute muscle injuries** associated with static stretching. The study was unable to conclude whether stretching reduced the risk of chronic, overuse injuries, which are the ones we encounter most often in active dogs.

3. Dynamic Stretching Effects on Performance

Dynamic stretching **improved performance overall by a minimal 1.3%**. It caused a 2.1% increase in jumping performance and a 1.4% improvement in running, sprinting, or agility. Dynamic stretching had an infinitesimal negative (-0.23%) effect on strength-based tasks such as maximal voluntary contractions.

4. Dynamic Stretching Effects on Injury Risk

No studies examined this question.

Dynamic stretches

The Bottom Line

Summarizing the findings, static stretching seems to reduce performance but also reduce the risk of acute muscle injuries. But again, **static stretching as part of a warm-up is irrelevant for dogs**. Dynamic stretching seems to minimally improve performance, and we don't know whether it is of benefit or not in reducing the risk of injuries.

If you want to include stretching as a component of your warm-up, just do dynamic stretching, in which your dog completes the action using muscular effort. Recognize, however, that the data suggest that even dynamic stretching has only a minimal beneficial effect on performance and an unknown positive or negative effect in reducing the risk of injuries.

The play bow is a good example of dynamic stretching for the front limbs and the spine. You can train your dog to initiate a play bow on its own by rewarding when those natural stretches occur. Or you can lure your dog into a play bow as shown in Figure 3.

An Appropriate Warm-Up Routine

Dynamic stretches are best done after the dog is slightly warmed up, so a good **warm-up program** for your dog would consist of:

1. Three to five minutes of **easy activity** such as walking around, trotting a bit, playing tug, etc., until your dog is open-mouthed breathing

2. **Optional dynamic stretches**, particularly those that flex and extend the spine ventrodorsally and laterally (Figure 3)

3. Activities that **briefly practice components** of the upcoming performance events, such as jumping, turning, fast starts, etc.

SPOTLIGHT

Figure 3. Spinal stretching exercises. Ventral flexion (top left), dorsal flexion (top right), lateral flexion (bottom left) with added rotation (bottom right).

For references, see Notes, p. 135.

7. Proprioception
Honing Your Dog's Injury-Prevention Skills

Proprio – what? Proprioception comes from the Latin *proprius*, meaning "one's own," and *capere*, meaning "to grasp." Thus, proprioception means **to grasp one's own position** in space, including the position of the limbs in relation to each other and the body as a whole. Proprioception is so important it is often called the 'sixth sense!'

Proprioception is how a baseball player hits a three-inch ball traveling at 95 mph with a 2¾-inch bat. It's how your agility dog flies over the dogwalk placing its feet in exactly the right spots. Check out Figure 1 – the dog's left rear foot has about one inch to spare! Proprioception is responsible for your dog's paw-eye and mouth-eye coordination. A well-tuned **proprioceptive system will prevent your dog from making missteps that could lead to a catastrophic injury**.

The neurological systems of mammals have sensory and motor components that control sensation and movement. But did you know that proprioception is a third nervous system component with its own nerves and pathways? That's how important it is!

Proprioception is so important that EVERY living thing has a proprioceptive system – mammals, birds, reptiles, and even insects. In fact, even plants have proprioception – it is how flowers know when open or close and to lean towards the sun for optimal energy production.

A Balancing Act
Your dog's proprioceptive system is like a body-wide GPS system. Just as your phone pings off cell phone towers to reveal where you are on the map, there are billions of sensors throughout your dog's body that constantly deliver neurological messages to your dog's brain. These sensors, also called *proprioceptors*, are present in the skin, muscles, tendons, and in tissues around the joints.

Figure 1. Foot placement is critical in many sports.

Your dog's proprioceptive system constantly delivers messages about body position to the brain.

Proprioceptors are tiny motion detectors that sense movements. They send messages along specialized nerve tracts to deliver information about the exact positions of every part of the body, as well as how fast and in what direction they are moving, and how much load they are bearing, so that instantaneous corrections can be made. So, if your dashing dog suddenly sees a divot in the ground, the proprioceptive system instantaneously moves your dog's foot to prevent a misstep. You can see why this system is so important in injury prevention!

At three weeks of age, as puppies are beginning to explore their world, they have more neurons than they will ever have. In their first months, neurons that are useful are retained and those that are unused are pruned and die off. For the proprioceptive neurological system to develop optimally, young puppies need to experience a lot of environmental stimuli (Figure 2). They need to move at varying speeds over different types of terrain and explore as many new objects as possible. That will help them retain all of those important proprioceptors, nerves, and spinal tracts.

It takes many months for a puppy's proprioceptive system to develop optimally. Remember how, as a fast-growing teenager, you kept bumping into things or were embarrassingly clumsy? The same is true for puppies as they grow. Sometimes the front legs are longer than they should be, then the rear legs or the body might grow and change the pup's proportions and balance. All this time, the proprioceptive system is scrambling to keep track of all these changes. Ultimately, at 1 to 1½ years of age, your dog knows what it's doing with its body, thanks to proprioception. This is one of the reasons why many people **recommend delaying intensive physical training until the body is mature to reduce the risk of injuries.**

Figure 2. A puppy developing proprioception.

Canine Activities That Get a Major Assist from Proprioception

Activity	How Proprioception Helps
Dogs having fun	Running safely over rough ground, avoiding groundhog holes, turning sharply and accurately, retrieving balls without sliding or rolling, playing chase games without tripping or banging into each other
Agility	Making accurate turns at speed, proper foot positions on contact obstacles, finding correct take-off spots for jumps, fast weave poles
Obedience	Straight fronts, finishes and sits, accurate heeling over poor footing on grass or over bumps in the mats
Rally	Faster, more accurate performance
Conformation	Optimal reach and drive when gaiting, smooth trot, fast, smooth set-up into stacked position
Hunt Tests/ Field Trials	Running safely over rough ground, avoiding obstacles and dips, turning sharply and accurately
Flyball	Faster runs, more accurate take-off positions, better ball retrieval, more accurate turns
IGP (IPO/Schutzhund)	More accurate, safer bite work, more accurate obedience, safer jumps, faster retrieves
Disc Dog	Safer, more accurate catches and landings
Dock Diving	Longer jumps because of better striding to reach the perfect take-off
Freestyle	Faster, more accurate performance, more precise trick behaviors

Tom Hills

Losing It

Unfortunately, "use it or lose it" seems to be the motto of the neurological system. As a result, it is important that dogs participate in activities and exercises throughout their lives to keep that proprioceptive system tuned up.

Here are **some instances when the proprioception system might go into decline**:
- **When a dog is injured** and must spend weeks or months with minimal exercise, the proprioceptive system loses its sharpness. This is one reason why a slow return to activity is recommended.
- **When your dog is tired**, proprioception is temporarily impaired. This is one reason why exercising your dog to exhaustion greatly increases the risk of injuries. See Chapters 9 and 12.
- **As your dog ages**, the proprioceptive system starts to lose its polish. However, studies of elderly and frail people have shown that strength and balance training help slow that process and reduce the risks of injuries.

Exercises to Hone Proprioception

All types of exercise give the proprioceptive system a workout. However, specific exercises can be used to more rapidly strengthen those pathways. Here are some:
- *Ladder Work.* Have your dog step VERY SLOWLY across the rungs of a ladder placed on the ground, first forward and then forward followed by backward. Make sure you use a ladder, not just cavaletti poles, because your dog needs to know where the sides of its feet are, not just the front and back.
- *Adventure Walks.* One of the best ways to tune up proprioception is to take your dog for off-leash hikes/walks over natural terrain – woods, washes, fields, etc. All your dog's joyful movements over different surfaces will work wonders for body awareness.
- *Circling.* Have your dog slowly turn in a tight circle to the right and left, two to three times in the same direction each time. Do your circles over various changes in the ground such as grass, gravel, hard top, sand, etc. Then put a few obstacles in the way, such as toys, balls, bottles, or ground poles, for your dog to avoid stepping on. Remember – have your dog clrcle SLOWLY so that their senses can experience all the changes in footing and position.

Interestingly, chiropractic work is specifically designed to hone proprioception, so getting regular adjustments should be a part of every active dog's maintenance routine (Figure 3).

Figure 3. Dog getting a chiropractic adjustment.

Just Do It!

Hopefully, you are convinced of the importance of the proprioceptive system in improving your dog's ability to experience a full and active life. Surprisingly, few people include proprioceptive exercises in their dogs' fitness regimens. That might be because these exercises seem…well…too simple. They don't get your dog panting or tire them out, so sometimes people believe they aren't that important. But in fact, **unseen neurological changes are taking place when your dog executes these exercises**.

Keeping your dog's proprioceptive system honed might be the most important thing you can do to reduce the risk of injuries, with all of their associated costs, downtime, and heartache. In addition, the scientific evidence suggests that **proprioceptive exercises are one of the best ways to increase your dog's health span** – the length of time your dog is healthy and active – and who doesn't want that? So just do it – only 10 minutes twice a week and you're good to go!

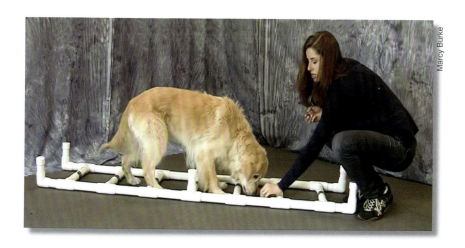

Marcy Burke

For references, see Notes, p. 135.

8. Overloaded
It's Not About Reps and Sets

Overload. Despite how it sounds, it is a critical factor to consider when building your dog's strength!

Strength is a major **key to canine health and longevity**. **A dog with strong muscles is less likely to suffer injuries**. That includes acute injuries such as strains and sprains, as well as chronic injuries such as arthritis, which is one of the most common painful conditions in senior and geriatric dogs. And of course, for those who enjoy training and competing with their dogs, **strength is strongly correlated with speed**, a component of many dog sports.

The **overload principle** is one of the major concepts of strength training. Simply put, it says that if you want to improve your dog's strength, you must progressively increase the **total work** that your dog's muscles perform.

What do we mean by **Total Work**? Total Work is a combination of the *frequency*, *duration*, and *intensity* that your dog experiences during exercise.

- **Frequency** is how often your dog does strength training.
- **Duration** is the length of time during which your dog works in each session.
- **Intensity** is more subjective and represents how physically difficult the exercise is.

Reps and Sets are Secondary

If you have ever worked out with a personal trainer, you have noticed that he or she will tell you to repeat an exercise a certain number of times. For example, let's say you are performing biceps curls to strengthen your biceps muscles. Your trainer might ask you to lift a 12-lb dumbbell 10 times. These are repetitions, or "reps." After a brief rest period, your trainer then tells you to perform another group of reps – perhaps eight biceps curls with a 15-lb dumbbell. Each of those groups of reps is called a "set."

Now, what you might not realize is that your trainer is carefully watching you and determining how many more reps of a specific weight will cause you to be unable to continue the reps near the end of a second or third set. That's **overload** – when you've done some exercise, but you can no longer continue. Your trainer knows that overload is necessary to build strength, and their goal is to guide you to that point.

An important concept of overload is that it should occur near the end of a period of progressively increasing total work. Continuing with the example of performing biceps curls, if your trainer asked you to do 100 reps with a 1-lb dumbbell, you are unlikely to go into overload at all. On the other hand, if he or she asks you to do biceps curls with a 30-lb dumbbell, you might be unable to do even one curl! Neither of those two scenarios will help strengthen your biceps.

As you can see from this example, the concept of overload is primary. Reps and sets are only used as a means to progressively increase the total work performed by the muscles to reach overload. Because each dog is an individual with different degrees of strength, **there is no standing rule regarding the number of reps or sets** that your dog should perform for any given exercise. **The number of reps or sets is determined on an individual basis for each dog as a way to work progressively to overload**.

How to Recognize Overload in Your Dog

When you are going into overload while exercising, your muscles might shake, you might grimace, and eventually you will fail to be able to perform the exercise. The signs of overload in dogs are similar, though often more subtle, and include:

- Shaking of the legs
- Quivering of the muscles
- Sudden distractibility
- Lack of effort
- Fidgeting
- Moving away
- Losing form

Furthermore, different exercises might induce different signs of overload. Watch your dog carefully and you will soon learn its individual signs of overload.

For example, when practicing having your dog sit on its haunches to improve core strength, when approaching overload your dog might fall to one side or put its front feet down. Or your dog might fall back onto the pelvis into a sloppy sitting position.

On the other hand, when you are working on diagonal leg lifts, another core strength exercise, overload is usually indicated by excessive fidgeting, or the dog just sitting down. Part of the fun of working strength exercises with your dog involves getting to know what overload looks like in your individual dog for any given exercise.

> *There is no rule regarding the number of reps or sets that your dog should perform for any given exercise.*

Rules for Safe Overloading

1. Progress gradually. It is better to take longer to build strength than to risk an injury.

2. Provide recovery time. Never strength train the same set of muscles two days in a row. Leave 48 hours for the muscles to recover. This will prevent overtraining, which can lead to injuries.

3. Keep a log of training sessions, briefly listing the frequency, duration, and intensity of the exercises you are asking your dog to perform. Also, make a note of your dog's behavior as it went into overload. That will help you recognize overload in the future so you can stop when overload occurs and not push your dog so hard that it becomes exhausted, which increases the risk of injury. Finally, note your dog's reaction to working to overload. Did your dog seem sore later? Extra tired? If so, you should back off on how hard you push to overload the next time.

> **QUICK TIP:**
> **Rules for Overloading**
> - Progress gradually
> - Provide recovery time
> - Keep records

Exceptions to the Overload Principle – Geriatric Dogs and Puppies

Geriatric dogs need to be exercised very carefully to prevent injury and maintain joy and motivation. While it is still useful to work these dogs to overload, stop at the very first sign of overload. In addition, if you have any indication at all that your dog is resisting the exercise, stop and rethink how you are performing the exercise and reevaluate whether your dog might be experiencing pain, such as that due to arthritis, rather than overload.

Puppies under six months of age should not be strength trained. Between six months and the age of growth plate closure (12 to 14 months in intact dogs, 18 to 22 months in dogs that were spayed or neutered pre-pubertally), puppies should only be gently strength-trained. Watch for the very earliest signs of overload and stop then. Puppy bodies are growing rapidly and changing shape and proportion. Let that growth and development happen without excessive emphasis on gaining muscular strength.

For references, see Notes, p. 135.

9. Build Stamina – Prevent Injuries

Stamina is often confused with endurance, but they are quite different.

Stamina is the strength and energy that allows your dog to sustain **physical** and/or **mental** effort for long periods of time (see Table below). Stamina is the opposite of fatigue. For example, your dog has great stamina if it can run at the same yards per second on the sixth agility run or the 20th flyball run of the day as it did on the first. Increasing your dog's stamina **reduces fatigue and exhaustion** and therefore helps prevent injuries. That's important to all of us, whether we have a performance, working, or family dog.

In contrast, **endurance** is the cardiopulmonary ability to perform a **continuous** motion over a long period of time. Mushing dogs that run upwards of 100 miles a day, and dogs that accompany their people on a several-mile run have good endurance. Endurance activities usually involve more moderate speeds than strength activities, but those speeds are sustained over a longer period. Of course, for a dog to run an endurance race of 100 miles, it must also have stamina.

To safely participate in strength activities repeatedly throughout the day, a dog needs stamina.

Strength/Endurance/Stamina Comparison

Strength Activities	Endurance Activities
Musculoskeletal	Cardiopulmonary
Faster speeds	Slower speeds
Stamina is the ability to participate in either of these activities over a long period of time.	

Discovering the Dog
Build Stamina

Strength and Endurance
Strength Activities

Although some dog activities require a combination of strength and endurance, most tend to be predominantly one or the other. Strength is most important for dogs that compete in agility, flyball, Fast CAT, obedience, rally, nosework/scent work, barn hunt, coursing, dock-diving, hunt tests, IGP, and most other popular dog sports. These activities all require strength – that is the ability to move the body at fast speeds for short distances, including running in short bursts, jumping, turning, etc.

To safely participate in strength activities repeatedly throughout the day, a dog needs stamina. Stamina is also important for dogs that accompany their people on hikes or just spend an active day with the family.

Endurance Activities

Mushing, bike-joring, and canicross are predominantly endurance sports. Less confusing terms for these activities are "cardiopulmonary" or "aerobic." Dogs whose people are avid long-distance runners also need cardiopulmonary or aerobic abilities. **Because of the length of time during which many of these activities occur, these dogs also need stamina.**

Here is a human sports-related comparison of strength and endurance. Think about runners who compete in the 100-m dash vs marathon runners (Figure 1). Usain Bolt has been clocked at an astounding 28 mph. That requires tremendous strength, and one look at the muscularity of his body confirms that. In contrast, competitive marathoners like Dennis Kimetto run at about 12-15 mph, but over a much more sustained period. That requires endurance. If Usain Bolt were to run multiple heats in a single day, he would require stamina. Because Dennis Kimetto runs for over two hours at a time, he also requires stamina.

Figure 1. Usain Bolt (left) and Dennis Kimetto (right). Note the differences in their body types.

If you build stamina, your dog will be able to exercise for a longer period of time before arriving at overload (Figure 2). That's important because when the muscles become exhausted, your dog enters the injury zone. In the injury zone, two different things can happen:

1. Your dog's weakening muscles allow greater-than-normal flexion and extension of the joints. This can lead to strains (stretch injury to the muscle and/or tendon) and/or sprains (stretch injury to ligaments).

2. Your dog is not able to be as careful about foot placement and might also not have the strength or speed to correct an error, like a foot that slips off the side of the agility dogwalk or off the edge of a cliff as your dog runs along a trail. These kinds of errors also increase the risk of injury.

Figure 2. Stamina can be increased by repeatedly building to overload but not past it, multiple times in one session and/or multiple times a day.

How to Increase Your Dog's Stamina

The best strength exercises are those that gradually work your dog to overload. For a detailed discussion of the overload principle see Chapter 8. **When your dog approaches overload**, depending on the exact motions that the exercise involves, you will begin to notice that **your dog starts to "cheat" a bit, either by changing its body position, moving away, fidgeting, or stopping entirely**. This is a sign that your dog's muscles are starting to fatigue, and that is a good time to stop the exercise. Record what you were doing when overload occurred (how many seconds or reps, depending on the exercise), so that next time you work on the exercise, you can start a little bit before that point with the goal of working past that point. In addition, keeping records will help you determine whether your dog is gaining strength. This is important, because if your dog isn't progressing, it's possible that your dog has an injury.

To boost your dog's stamina, work an exercise to overload three to four times in a session, taking a 90-second break each time your dog reaches overload. Another way to increase stamina is to work the exercise to overload several times a day. You can alternate between these two methods or do both in a single day. It's as simple as that!

By building stamina, you will greatly reduce the risk of injury when your dog is training, competing or just being a happy dog playing with you or other dogs. It's a win-win for everyone!

10. Reducing Injury Risk:
The Facts!

Does fitness training really reduce the risk of injuries? Everyone says so, but **what's the proof**? And if so, **what kind of exercise is most effective**? Strength? Proprioception (body awareness)? Stretching? Let's take a look at **the evidence**.

First, it is important to note that **published research studies have different levels of validity**. There is an established **hierarchy of evidence** (see figure below), with systematic reviews of randomized placebo-controlled clinical trials providing the strongest evidence, and editorials/expert opinion providing the weakest evidence. Note that Facebook posts don't even appear in the hierarchy ☺.

The Hierarchy of Evidence

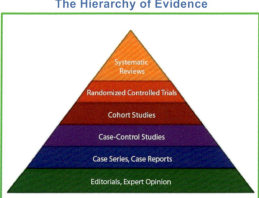

There is no systematic review of clinical trials that has examined the ability of canine fitness programs to reduce the risk of injuries. But there have been several in humans. It is valid to **apply the results of human studies to dogs** because the musculoskeletal systems of the two species are very similar. **Human studies might even be better** because people can be given detailed instructions for how to complete specific exercises, thus providing good fidelity to the results.

A systematic review (a study of the validity, bias, and consistency of the results of a group of studies) of the role of strength training in **reducing injuries has been published**. It examined six randomized clinical trials involving 7,738 participants to determine whether there is any relationship between strength training and acute and/or overuse injury. The authors determined that these six studies had appropriate controls and statistical evidence and revealed no evidence of bias. The authors concluded that:

1. Strength training significantly reduced the risk of acute and overuse injuries by about 66%.

2. The higher the total volume of exercise, measured by repetitions (reps), the **greater the reduction in injury risk**

3. Working to muscle overload was more effective in reducing injury risk than a pre-determined number of reps.

A previous systematic review revealed that **both strength and proprioceptive exercises reduce injury risk**, but that stretching did not. The finding that proprioceptive exercises reduce the risk of injury was also confirmed by another study.

How do strength and proprioception training reduce injury risk? A brain study was undertaken to address this very question. Ten female soccer players underwent fMRI (imaging that shows which parts of the brain are being used) during the preseason. During the soccer season, two of the 10 athletes sustained injuries to their anterior cruciate ligaments. The fMRI studies showed that the **athletes who did not get injured had significantly better connections** between the area of the brain where **voluntary movement** (which is governed by strength) is initiated and the area that is responsible for **balance and coordination** (proprioception). That study helps to demonstrate the importance of strength and proprioception exercises to reduce the risk of injury in our dogs. Some examples of strength and proprioception exercises are shown in the table below.

Examples of Strength and Proprioception Exercises*

Front Leg Strength	Core Strength	Rear Leg Strength	Proprioception
Wave	Beg	Rear Leg Targeting	The Ladder
High-9s	Diagonal Leg Lifts	Front Feet Perched	Walk the Plank
Handstand	Sit-Stand-Sit	Walking a Peanut Ball	Backing Up

There is strong evidence that strength and proprioceptive exercises reduce injury.

*A flash drive with videos demonstrating these exercises and many more can be purchased here: https://caninesports.com/product/ffl-videos/ or videos can be live streamed individually here: https://vimeo.com/ondemand/caninefitforlife

For references, see Notes, p. 135.

11. Stop Taking Your Dog for a Walk!
(Try a Saunter Instead)

Pretty well everyone agrees that taking your dog for a walk is just about the best exercise for your dog, right? Maybe… or maybe not.

What is Exercise Anyway?
There are two broad categories of outdoor exercise – those that improve or maintain our dogs' fitness, and those that are just good for the soul.

The components of fitness exercise are **strength**, **proprioception**, **balance**, **flexibility**, and **endurance**. So, let's analyze whether walks, in fact, make our dogs fitter.

Do Walks Build Strength?

The focus of strength exercise is to build muscle size and tone. Strong muscles will allow your dog to safely do whatever kind of physical exercise he or she enjoys, whether that means competing in performance events or running through a forest while on a hike. A dog that is strong will be less likely to experience an acute injury when something unexpected happens. It also will be less likely to develop chronic conditions such as arthritis because its strength will help reduce the effects of repeated impact on the body.

The science of strength training for humans is very clear. To build strength, it is important to engage in exercises that will:

- **Target** parts of the body that need improvement, such as the arms, core, or legs.
- Be as **low impact** as possible.
- Work to muscle failure or **overload**, but not exhaustion.

Taking your dog for an invigorating walk provides him or her with none of the above three characteristics. It **doesn't target** the weakest parts of your dog's body, it is certainly **not low impact**, and it is exceedingly **difficult to recognize when your dog has reached overload**, though it is clear when they have reached exhaustion, because they slow down and don't want to participate any more.

Try a saunter instead of a march.

Do Walks Improve Proprioception?
Proprioception is all about body awareness – understanding where all the parts of the body are in space (Chapter 7). Proprioception is so important that there are specific neurological pathways that send neurological impulses from proprioceptive receptors in the skin and soft tissues, up the spinal cord to the brain to help direct the body's movements. To improve proprioception, it is best to provide the body with a wide variety of different types of movements and surfaces to walk on.

Walking on a sidewalk or city street does little to improve proprioception.

A walk on a city street or sidewalk does little to improve proprioception. But a walk on different types of surfaces such as long and short grass, gravel, dirt, wood chips, etc. does improve proprioception by providing different substrates for the proprioceptors in the feet to contact. That's especially true if the dog is going slowly enough for the feet to be in contact with the different surfaces for a while.

Do Walks Improve Balance?
Much like proprioception, balance training strengthens your dog's neurological system, which helps your dog negotiate complex movements and react safely when put in an unexpected situation.

A walk over a consistent surface like a sidewalk or mowed lawn doesn't provide much challenge to your dog's balance system. A hike over rocky or hilly ground does.

Do Walks Make Your Dog More Flexible?
Flexibility allows the muscles to fully flex and extend the muscles over their working lengths without overstretching and risking damage. Clearly, during a typical walk, your dog doesn't fully flex or extend its limbs.

Are Walks an Aerobic Exercise for Dogs?
Aerobic exercise involves moving in a way that will get the heart and respiratory rate elevated over a period of time. Dogs' muscles are different from those of humans. The system that provides energy to your dog's muscles is already highly aerobic. To improve on your dog's inbuilt aerobic abilities, your dog should trot at a consistent, at least moderate, speed for at least 20 minutes or swim at a consistent speed for at least five minutes.

Most people taking their dogs for a walk are not able to walk fast enough for long enough to really improve their dog's aerobic capabilities unless the dog is a pretty small tyke, like under 20 lb. But there's good news on the aerobic front! Since dogs are already such aerobic machines, they really don't need much help in this area unless they are competing in mushing, canicross, field trials, or herding trials. So, for most of you, strength and stamina training are all you need.

Going for a Walk – Your Dog's Point of View
Try this thought experiment. Imagine yourself at less than half your human height, with four legs, a furry body, a wagging tail, and an incredible sense of smell. Now, imagine yourself running, bounding, walking, and resting at times, on a path in a forest, jumping over logs, rolling in a pile of dry leaves, listening to the different bird calls, playing in a trickling brook, and smelling the scents of moist soil, moss, old, crumbling logs and all of the animals that have passed that way for weeks. This feels so good for your soul!

Next, imagine yourself attached to a 6-foot leash, walking on hardtop in a straight line at the constant speed of your person, who is looking straight ahead, listening to music on their earphones. You would like to stop and sniff, maybe send a pee-mail note or two to the neighborhood, but you are whisked past these tantalizing odors. Your feet are pounding on the pavement, and while you love being with your person, you sure wish that she would look down at you, which always makes you feel better.

Delphine Beausoleil

How About a Compromise?

The literature is rife with the benefits to people, particularly the elderly, who take their dogs for walks. The science is clear that moving is one of the healthiest things you can do for yourself. Walking your dog, in addition to providing exercise, increases the likelihood that you will exercise in other ways as well. One study showed that older adults with dogs took more steps, burned more calories, were less likely to be obese, and got more and better sleep than non-dog people. Dogs are also great social catalysts, so they increase interactions between people, which is an important benefit for everyone. So, if you want to reap the benefits of exercise by walking your dog, by all means do so in moderation, but recognize that, depending on how you go for a walk, you might be the main one benefitting, rather than your dog. If you plan on going for a multi-mile march with your earphones on, consider whether it might be better for your dog to stay home.

Patrick Schatz

If you truly want to give your dog the gift of a walk, enjoyed from your dog's point of view, take him or her for a saunter. Dress yourself and your dog for the weather, attach a long line (12 feet or four meters works well), and head out to the very best that nature in your locale can offer.

Saunter on grass, through fields and forests (off leash if possible), or along the sidewalk at your dog's pace, stopping to sniff as long as they want, send numerous group pee-mail messages, watch the squirrels tease them from the trees, and expect to go nowhere important. That is one of the greatest gifts you can give your dog – it is so good for their soul. And you might just find it's good for yours, too.

For references, see Notes, p. 136.

12. Play Ball!...Safely
Co-Authored by Gayle Watkins PhD*

Cody strained at his leash as he entered my examination room. A brown and white Pitbull mix with soft eyes, large neck and shoulder muscles, and a beautiful sheen to his coat, he rubbed the side of his big body against my legs then flipped over onto his back, begging for a belly rub. His tongue lolled to one side of his mouth, and he sported a silly grin. On the inside of his left knee, I could see a prominent scar from a recent surgery.

Cody had ruptured his cranial cruciate ligament (CCL), a structure that supports the knee joint, about four months previously. He had endured expensive surgery and lengthy rehabilitation to stabilize his knee in the hopes of reducing the chance that he would develop severe arthritis, and to help him to have a pain-free life. Cody and his person were consulting with me to arrange a conditioning and retraining program to enable him to safely return to all the activities he loved.

After examining Cody and prescribing some exercises to rebuild his core and hind limb musculature, Cody's person asked, "When can he play ball again? That's his favorite thing to do!"

As I considered my answer, I thought about Harper, who came in last week with lumbosacral disease, which caused weakness and back pain. Her person brought me a video showing her dog leaping for a frisbee and landing on her rear legs, back hyperextended as she tried to capture that hovering object.

I recalled the many dogs who come to me with CCL ruptures, iliopsoas strains, and bulging lumbosacral disks and how often their people tell me that their dogs love to retrieve.

At home that evening, I watched my crazy Golden Retriever slide on the grass and then do a 360-degree turn as he tried to grab his ball, despite the fact that I had thrown it far enough that it was stationary when he reached it.

---

*Dr. Gayle Watkins has been breeding Golden Retrievers under the Gaylan's prefix for over 40 years. She has been selected as an AKC Sport Breeder of the Year four times in four different sports. Since 2012, Gayle has run Avidog, the online "university" for dog breeders and puppy owners, which she co-founded.

What Is It About Retrieving?
What is it about retrieving that makes many dogs (and their people) lose their minds, completely forgetting self-preservation and control? After delving a bit deeper into canine behavior and neurology, I think I have a better handle on that conundrum.

When you throw a ball, you are stimulating your dog's prey drive and innate instinct to chase. Your dog cannot help himself – he **must** overtake that moving object! Why? Ray and Lorna Coppinger, biologists, breeders, trainers, and champion sled dog racers with decades of experience with thousands of dogs, consider retrieving to be an instinctual behavior. Like other instinctual behaviors (sex, eating, and scenting), **chase and catch are internally rewarding and provide deep joy, contentment, and optimism to many dogs**.

Coppinger says, "If a dog gets pleasure out of performing (a behavior), it keeps looking for places to display it. The animal will search for the releaser of (the behavior) because it gets rewarded so luxuriously for performing." In this case, you are the releaser, the giver of this luxurious reward, so "a good retriever sits there and begs you to throw the ball again."

In addition, **we also are rewarded**, because the game of retrieving is relational. **You** are the person who gives this gift to your dog and the dog seeks to experience this joy through you. When our dogs are happy, we are happy. This must be a good thing, right? How wonderful to be able to give our dogs the gift of joy!

Too Much of a Good Thing?
From a neurological point of view, the **chemical messenger responsible for that feeling of bliss is dopamine**. It's the same neurotransmitter that gives you that ever-so-brief but wonderful feeling at your first taste of a delicious food and during happy sex. Recent studies suggest, however, that not only does dopamine provide that blissful feeling, it also **drives the individual to seek that feeling over and over**. That is why drugs like cocaine that cause dopamine release are so addictive.

Likewise, **when your dog experiences dopamine release during the chase and catch, he wants more, and more, and more**. And when your dog brings the ball back to you, you see those bright eyes, and that body leaping and begging for you to throw the object again and it is clear that your dog loves this game! Maybe you get a bit of dopamine release too! And so, you throw again, and again, and again.

When your dog experiences that dopamine release during the chase, he wants more.

However, more is happening to your dog's body than just a flood of dopamine while retrieving. During the chase, your dog is highly aroused. Her eyelids are wide open, her pupils are dilated, and her muscles are tensed for action. Adrenaline is coursing through her veins and the entire sympathetic nervous system is on high alert. **When the ball moves, she MUST chase!** She is not thinking about the tree, or the ditch, or the suddenly approaching car. She doesn't care whether she must leap off a wall, slide on some gravel, or spread-eagle to snag the ball. And **if she does get injured, she won't feel any pain. At least not until later**. That's adrenaline for you!

The Injury Zone

As your dog retrieves the first…second…third…maybe fifth or sixth ball, his **muscles start to tire and soon they reach overload, where they no longer can fully control and support your dog's movements**. Now, when your dog does those amazing athletic maneuvers to snag the ball, soft tissues like the cranial cruciate ligament, iliopsoas muscle and tendon, and the muscles and ligaments that support the vertebrae are overstretching. Minor tears are occurring. Now the ball is thrown 10, 12 times or more and ultimately your dog lies down, exhausted.

That period between when your dog's muscles are in overload, and when your dog lies down exhausted, is the injury zone (Figure 1). But remember, with all that adrenaline, your dog doesn't feel the injuries happening, so you have no idea that the tissues are being used beyond their capacity.

When this game is repeated day after day, month after month, the small tissue tears become large ones, and suddenly it becomes evident that your dog is in pain and has an injury. Of course, it hasn't been sudden at all – what seemed sudden is just the final result of repeated stress and strain until the tissues gave way.

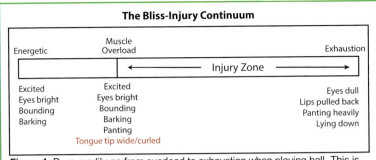

Figure 1. Dogs readily go from overload to exhaustion when playing ball. This is when injuries are more likely to happen.

How To Play Ball Safely

The key to safe retrieving is to stop your dog when it arrives at the point of muscle overload, just like you should stop yourself from reaching for a second bag of chips, no matter how good the first bag tasted.

How do you recognize overload? **Watch your dog's tongue**. When the tip of the tongue becomes wider and/or curls up, that is your signal that your dog has just used her final mechanism to dissipate body heat. And that's a pretty good indicator that your dog has reached muscle overload. So, even if that happens on the second retrieve, be the grown-up, stop the game and make sure your dog is in a cool place to rest and recover. In conclusion, don't use the retrieve to tire your dog out. Use it to give your dog joy.

Don't use the retrieve to tire your dog out. Use it to give your dog joy.

On the next page is a list of additional parameters you can institute to make the retrieving game safer for your dog. Your dog will have just as much fun with these rules in place. You might have to teach other family members these rules, and enforce them, but in the long term, they are worth it.

How to Play Ball Safely

1. Throw the ball/toy/disc and/or release your dog in such a way that the **object will be stationary** when your dog reaches it. Or throw the object into cover so that your dog must search for it.

2. **Never have your dog catch a thrown object in the air**, unless you are training or competing in disc dog and have trained your dog to properly land on the front legs after catching.

3. Provide your dog with the right balance of **strength, balance, and body awareness exercises** so that he or she will be physically prepared for the extreme exercise that repeated retrieving requires.

4. Use **balls** that are:
- Small enough to be easily caught but not so small as to be a choking hazard
- Grippy, not slippery
- Do not have just one hole (no holes or two or more holes are fine)

For references, see Notes, p. 136.

13. No Hot Dogs Please!

Not the kind you eat – you can make your own decisions about that! I'm talking literally: hot… dogs.

Maybe you are thinking, "Oh gosh, I already know everything about this topic: Don't leave your dog in the car, dogs have less efficient cooling mechanisms than people, blah, blah, blah." Well, bear with me, because there are a couple of studies that just might surprise you. In fact, they just might **save your dog's life**.

How Do Dogs Overheat?
There are just two ways your dog can become a hot dog – due to external or internal factors.

External Factors. This is the cause of overheating that we think of most often – dogs exposed to high temperatures and/or humidity, such as dogs left in cars or left out in a yard without shade.

Internal Factors. Exercise generates heat. Muscle contraction and movement of the musculoskeletal system produce a tremendous amount of heat! In one study, **physical activity was more important than temperature or humidity in contributing to heatstroke**. Of course, if your dog is exercising in hot/humid temperatures, the risk of heat stroke is greatly amplified!

The Discomfort Index
There is a formula that takes temperature and humidity into account and produces a number called the Discomfort Index, or DI. You can find a DI calculator at this link: https://keisan.casio.com/exec/system/1351058230. Just plug in the current temperature and humidity and it will give you the corresponding DI – pretty cool (or maybe not)! One study showed that dogs are quite comfortable when the DI is less than 22, they are moderately uncomfortable when the DI is 22 to 28 and very uncomfortable when it is above 28.

How Do Dogs Cool?
We all know that the most important cooling system for dogs is evaporation of moisture from the upper respiratory tract – the mouth, nasal passages, pharynx, larynx, etc. A second, much less efficient, cooling mechanism is by dilating the blood vessels under the skin and expelling the heat from the vascular system through the skin. However, dogs do not have very many blood vessels under the skin over much of their body, with the exception of the groin area. That is the best place to target if you need to take advantage of this cooling mechanism in a dog that is suffering from hyperthermia.

Why Are Some Dogs More Susceptible to Heat?

1. *Genetics*. Susceptibility to overheating is partly genetic. A study of elite and poor-performing Alaskan Huskies identified a single region in the genome that was associated with heat tolerance.

2. *Physical structure*. Physical characteristics are also associated with the ability of dogs to cool. In one study, brachycephalic dogs (dogs with short faces, such as Pugs, Shih Tzu, etc.) were shown to have poorer cooling mechanisms than dogs with longer noses. This is not surprising given that brachycephalic breeds have a shorter upper respiratory tract and often have folds of extra tissue in the oropharynx that can interfere with air flow.

3. *Body condition*. The more surprising result of the above study was that **being overweight was a bigger factor than brachycephaly in a dog's inability to cool**. The higher the dog's body condition score, using the Purina BCS system, the warmer they got during exercise, and the lower their tidal volume (air flow into the lungs) was. In addition, obese dogs are more likely to die if they do experience heatstroke. There's yet another reason to keep your dog fit!

Track Your Dog's Heat Susceptibility

Keep a record of your dog's heat susceptibility. This is a simple matter of recording the following each time you take your dog outside:

- Date and time
- Temperature, humidity and DI
- Number of minutes of exercise
- Strenuousness of exercise (on a scale of 1 to 3)
- Dog's distress level (on scale of 1 to 3, where 1 is slightly panting, 2 is moderate panting, and 3 is panting with the tongue enlarged and/or curled at the end)

After a few outings, you'll have a pretty good idea of how much of what type of exercise will be best for your individual dog given the current DI.

What Is The Best Way to Cool a Dog?

A recent study compared three mechanisms for cooling dogs after a 15-min treadmill exercise in a room at 30° C (86° F). Dogs that were dipped in water at ambient temperature for five minutes cooled to a normal body temperature in 16 minutes. Dogs that were placed in a kennel on a cooling mat at 4° C (39° F) with a fan took 36 minutes to cool. Dogs that were just in a kennel with a fan took 48 minutes to cool down.

The authors suggested that water immersion is an excellent method for not only treating, but also for preventing overheating when dogs exercise. They suggested having a dipping tank available whenever dogs are doing intensive activities that might put them at risk for heatstroke.

This is a great reason for clubs or outdoor training facilities to purchase a pool or stock tank large enough to submerge dogs if there is no access to air conditioning.

For references, see Notes, p. 136.

14. Star Light, Star Bright
Emerging Evidence that Light Therapy Can Improve Sports Performance

You've likely heard of the healing effects of laser therapy. There is abundant, peer-reviewed scientific evidence that light can penetrate the skin and cell membranes and enter mitochondria (the energy producing factories of the cell). There, the light energy is converted into adenosine tri-phosphate (ATP), the form of energy that the cell uses for healing. This is a photochemical effect comparable to photosynthesis in plants whereby light is absorbed by a leaf and undergoes a chemical change to provide energy for the plant.

We shouldn't be surprised that light has power. We know, for example, that sunlight kills some bacteria. Although laser technology was invented in the early 1960s, recently the field has exploded with studies demonstrating the healing effects of light therapy, now officially referred to as photobiomodulation therapy (PBMT). Hundreds of peer-reviewed studies show that PBMT can promote tissue regeneration, reduce inflammation, and relieve pain in injured soft tissues such as muscles, tendons, and ligaments.

Just in the last few years studies have revealed that PBMT can even improve hard-to-treat neurological and psychological conditions such as stroke, traumatic brain injury, Parkinson's disease, and depression.

There is growing evidence that PBMT improves muscle strength and enhance sports-related performance. That's crazy you say? Let's take a closer look at those studies.

First, Some Background
No one hates physics more than I do but, in fact, it is quite interesting (and simple) when we are talking about how PBMT works. So here are a few FAQs about PBMT:

1. What forms of light can be used for PBMT?
Only light in the infrared or near infrared wavelengths (600 to 1,064 nm) can be converted by the cell into energy. These wavelengths of light can be produced by lasers or LEDs. The main difference between the two is that lasers produce more photons, and they are all aimed in one direction, whereas LEDs produce fewer photons that are emitted multidirectionally.

2. That's a wide range of wavelengths. What's the difference between wavelengths?
In general, the longer the wavelength, the deeper into the tissue the light penetrates.

3. Since PBMT is a type of therapy, how are doses measured?
When dosing with light, we use a unit of energy called the *joule* (J). One watt (W), or 1000 milliwatts (mW) of power, produces one joule of energy per second. So, a typical laser with a power of 500 mW will produce one joule every two seconds. On the other hand, one LED light in a string of holiday lights has a power of approximately 70 mW, so it will take about 14 seconds for one of those lights to produce one joule of energy. When applying light therapy to a tissue, we describe dose exposure in J/cm^2.

A dog receiving laser therapy

Studies of the Effects of PBMT on Performance
The hierarchy of evidence (see Chapter 10) indicates that the best evidence consists of systematic reviews of randomized clinical trials. It just so happens that there is a systematic review of randomized clinical trials examining the effects of PBMT on human sports performance. So helpful!

That study reviewed 46 randomized, placebo-controlled clinical trials that included 1,045 participants. It concluded that **PBMT can increase muscle mass gained after training and decrease inflammation and oxidative stress in muscles**. They postulate that these effects are related to the fact that PBMT is known to increase ATP, the biological source of energy needed for muscle work. The review quotes many different studies that show improved performance of various muscle groups in humans.

As an example, let's discuss one of the most practical, real-world studies – one that examined the effects of PBMT on the performance of high-level rugby players.

In that study, 12 male, world-class rugby players were treated with PBMT or placebo then run seven times through a timed sprint test that included turns, much like a dog agility course. PBMT significantly improved the average time for all sprints as well as measured and perceived fatigue, and blood lactate levels (a by-product of muscle energy metabolism). Pretty cool!

Can I Start Using Laser Therapy to Improve My Dog's Performance?

Despite growing evidence of the benefits of PBMT on sports performance, there are many questions to be answered before you can magically use laser or LED to turn your favorite furry athlete into a super canine star. They are:

- What is the best wavelength to use?
- Is it better to apply PBMT to muscles before or after exercise?
- How long should the time interval between light therapy and exercise be?
- How many sites of irradiation should be used and on which muscle groups?
- What are the best power (mW) and dose (J/cm^2) to use?
- How much does the dog's haircoat impede transmission of light?

The question of **dosing is especially important** because you might be thinking, "If low doses are beneficial, higher doses must be even more so!" Unfortunately, that is not the case. Numerous studies have shown that low doses of PBMT are beneficial, but higher doses can have no effect or might, in fact, be harmful. This biological process is called *hormesis* (Figure 1), just so you can impress your friends with your vocabulary. In any case, this little detail makes knowing the appropriate dose of PBMT very important!

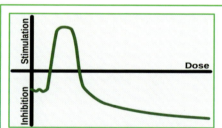

Figure 1. This graph shows the hormesis effect, in which a low or moderate dose of photobiomodulation therapy) results in a positive effect, but as the dose becomes higher, there is a negative therapeutic effect.

If low doses are beneficial, higher doses must be even more so! Unfortunately, that is not the case.

Another important question to be answered is: **how can we apply these bare-skinned human studies to our hairy dogs**? How do we know how much of the light source will penetrate a dog's coat to get to the skin? A laser treatment can be applied by hand, parting the coat and ensuring that the skin is exposed to the light, but ideally the dog should be shaved to get the full effect of the light that is emitted. This is even more true for LED products, which usually consist of arrays of small LEDs in a stiff or flexible casement. The internet abounds with LED products that claim to treat a variety of problems in dogs (based loosely on the effects of PBMT in humans), but not one accounts for light penetration through the fur. In fact, there are even concerns with penetration of laser light through fur. With so many different densities of fur in different breeds, this is an important issue. Perhaps we should only use LED arrays on Chinese Crested Dogs or Xoloitzcuintlis!

An additional confounding factor is the fact that **the darker the skin, the less the light penetrates to the tissues below**. This factor also has only been studied in humans, not dogs. So. if you have a hairy, dark-skinned dog, how much of the light is going to penetrate to the tissues where you want it to have its effect? We don't know, but some have suggested less than 5%. At this point, at least for dogs, PBMT to improve performance is not quite ready for primetime.

Despite all these cautions, however, the evidence is quite convincing that, if you can get light of the right wavelength and power to penetrate to the muscle, it has the potential to significantly improve your dog's athletic performance. The data in humans are so convincing that some studies suggest that PBMT should be placed on the World Anti-Doping Agency's list of prohibited substances, although how they will know whether a person has been treated has yet to come to light!

Thinking of Purchasing a Laser?

This is one place where the expression "**let the buyer beware**" has never been truer. Many companies sell lasers that are completely ineffective for treating your dog's injuries. After all, you can use a laser pointer when giving a presentation or to play with your cat, but it certainly wouldn't be effective in healing your dog's iliopsoas strain!

Bottom Line:

Expect to pay several thousand dollars for a Class IIIB laser with a minimum of 500 mW power and then to learn in detail how to use it. Before purchasing, you absolutely should discuss your purchase wtih a veterinarian certified in rehabilitation therapy.

Respond Systems

For references, see Notes, p. 137.

15. Do the Dewclaws?

A dog using its dewclaws to try to grip the water

As a veterinary sports medicine specialist, I work extensively with canine athletes, developing rehabilitation programs for injured dogs or dogs after required surgery due to performance-related injuries. I have seen many dogs, especially field trial/hunt test and agility dogs, that have chronic carpal arthritis, frequently so severe that they must be retired or at least carefully managed for the rest of their lives. I noticed that very few of those dogs had front dewclaws and began to wonder whether these appendages might, in fact, protect a dog from injuries. What I learned might surprise you.

The Anatomy of Dewclaws
Miller's Guide to the Anatomy of the Dog, a veterinary anatomy text, has an excellent figure depicting the muscular anatomy of the distal forelimb. There are two functional muscles, the *extensor pollicis longus et indicis proprius* and the *flexor digitorum profundus* that are attached to the front dewclaw by four tendons (Figure 1). Each of those muscle/tendon units has a different function in movement. That means that **if you cut off the dewclaws, you are preventing the muscles that were attached to the dewclaws from functioning**.

In contrast, rear limb dewclaws do not have muscle/tendon attachments, so their removal might be appropriate, except in the breeds such as Briards and Beauceron in which the breed standard states that they should be retained.

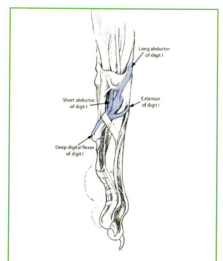

Figure 1. Anatomical diagram of the medial (inside) side of a dog's left front leg demonstrating four tendons that attach to the dewclaw. Illustration by M. Schlehr, from Miller's Guide to the Dissection of the Dog.

Figure 2. In this galloping dog, the left front dewclaw is in contact with the ground. If the dog needs to turn to the right, the dewclaw will dig into the ground to stabilize the lower leg and prevent torque.

Dewclaws Do Have Functions
If there are muscles and tendons attached to the dewclaws, then they most likely have a function. Broadly speaking, the front dewclaws have at least two different functions:

1. Grasping the ground when the dog is turning to prevent torque on the forelimb. Each time the front foot lands on the ground, particularly when the dog is cantering or galloping (Figure 2), the dewclaw is in contact with the ground. If the dog then needs to turn, **the dewclaw actively digs into the ground to stabilize the lower leg** and prevent torque. In Figure 3 you can clearly see the dewclaw of a Corgi herding a sheep extended, ready to grip the ground.

If a dog doesn't have dewclaws, the leg will twist on its axis, creating increased pressure, especially on the carpal bones, but also on the elbow, shoulder, and toes. A lifetime of this kind of torque can result in carpal arthritis or injuries to and subsequent arthritis in other joints of the forelimb. Remember, the dog is participating in the activity regardless, so there will be concussive pressures on the leg, and if the dewclaw is not there to help stabilize the leg, those pressures will be transmitted to other areas of the leg, especially the joints.

2. Gripping objects. We have all seen dogs using their dewclaws to grip objects such as balls or bones (Figure 4). I've even seen many photos of agility dogs gripping the teeter (Figure 5). But **did you know that the dewclaws' gripping ability can, in fact, save your dog's life?** Check out the video "Dewclaws Do Have a Purpose" at https://www.youtube.com/watch?v=r4XflsMEk-k&t=9s for 'gripping' views of

Figure 3. Corgi using its left front dewclaw while herding.

Figure 4. Dog using its left front dewclaw to grip a food toy.

dogs attempting to get out of water onto ice without the help of those ice picks on the insides of their legs. The video also shows dogs using their dewclaws to grip the ice and escape from a potentially fatal situation. I have known several dogs that drowned after falling through ice in the winter. None of them had dewclaws. If they had, perhaps they would have survived and spared their people the incredible heartache of watching their dogs die unnecessarily.

Arguments for Removing Dewclaws

1. The dewclaws will get injured. This is the most common reason I hear for removing dewclaws. A friend of mine had such a severe dewclaw injury in one of her dogs that she swore she would remove them on all the dogs she bred subsequently.

But the data indicate that, at least in agility dogs, **dewclaws are not injured very often**. One study showed that the dewclaw was the **least likely toe to be injured in agility dogs**, in which landing and turning from jumps and other obstacles put the toes at risk for injuries (see Chapter 16). Not only that, **dogs lacking dewclaws were more likely to injure the other toes**. Thus, it makes no sense to remove the dewclaws to reduce the risk of injury. No one would consider removing the 5th digits of the front feet (the toes on the outside), which are by far the most commonly injured toe, so why do we feel that dewclaws are dispensable?

2. People forget to trim the dewclaws. Surely this is a matter of education. Do we really want to remove a functioning digit in all dogs, just because some people need to be reminded that they must trim the dewclaws?

3. Dewclaws make the forelimb look less straight when viewed from the front in conformation. The AKC states: "The breed standard describes the characteristics of the ideal dog to perform the function for which it was bred." While we could have long discussions about the veracity of this statement, it is interesting to note that there are **very few breed standards that require dewclaw remova**l. I know of only one – the Vizsla breed standard.

A Plea:

Here's a plea to retain dogs' dewclaws. They are a functioning digit. They are the toe least likely to be injured. Isn't this enough to convince us not to do the dewclaws?

Figure 5. Kelpie using its left front dewclaw to grip the teeter for stability.

For references, see Notes, p. 138.

16. Digit Injuries

Sheltie using its left dewclaw to help make a sharp turn in the weave poles.

A retrospective study examined **digit injuries in dogs training and competing in agility**. The goal of the study was to identify potential risk factors for digit injuries in these dogs. The study used an extensive, internet-based survey in which owners/handlers were asked questions related to the nature of their dogs' digit injuries, their dogs' physical description including the feet, possible causes and circumstances of the injuries, the dogs' agility training and performance characteristics, and dog and owner demographic information. Confirmation of a digit injury by a veterinarian was not required. Completed surveys were received for 207 dogs with digit injuries and 874 dogs without.

The **5th digits (outside toes) were the most commonly injured** (Figure 1 shows how the digits are numbered), and those injuries were twice as common in the front feet as the rear feet. The two most common injuries of any toe were fractures (32.5% of injuries) and sprains/strains (27.8%).

Dewclaws were the least commonly injured digit (occurring in only 7.3% of dogs that had dewclaws).

After performing a multivariable logistic regression analysis, which takes into account the effects that multiple contributing factors might have on the outcome, **the following factors were associated with significantly increased odds of a digit injury**:

- **Being a Border Collie** (Odds Ratio, 2.4). This means that Border Collies were 2.4 times more likely to experience a toe injury than other breeds.

Figure 1. The numbered digits of a puppy's right front foot.

The dewclaws were the least commonly injured digit.

55 Discovering the Dog
Digit Injuries

- Having **long nails** (Odds Ratio = 2.4)
- **Not having front dewclaws** (Odds Ratio = 1.9)
- **Higher weight-to-height ratio** (Odds Ratio = 1.5)

The following factor was associated with significantly decreased odds of injury:
- **Increasing age** of the dog (Odds Ratio = 0.8)

> **How to decrease the likelihood of digit injuries:**
> - Retain the dewclaws
> - Maintain lean body mass
> - Trim nails short for training and competition

Not having front dewclaws was associated with a greater risk of injury to the other digits.

For references, see Notes, p. 138.

17. A-Frame-Induced Carpal Injuries?

Studies of injuries in agility dogs have suggested that the A-frame might contribute to agility-related injuries. One study examined the angle of the carpal (wrist) joint when dogs were ascending the A-frame. The goal of that study was **to determine whether lowering the height of the A-frame**, thus reducing the angle at which the A-frame meets the ground, **would reduce the amount of carpal extension** that dogs experience when ascending the obstacle.

The results showed that **regardless of whether the A-frame was positioned at angles of 30, 35 or 40 degrees to the ground, the dogs' carpi always extended to about 62 degrees** (Figure 1). The authors compared this angle to studies showing that maximal carpal angles in dogs walking on flat surfaces were 26 degrees, and in dogs traversing a jump were 44 degrees. They concluded that the carpal angles they measured in dogs ascending the A-frame represented maximal carpal extension. They suggested, as others have, that repetitive maximal carpal extension could damage soft tissue structures that support the carpus.

This was very **well-designed study** using a large number of dogs (n = 40) of a wide variety of breeds, and it asks a very important question about repetitive injuries. The data are very solid. However, my conclusions are slightly different than the authors'.

Figure 1. This figure from the publication shows how the angle of each dog's carpus as it ascended the A-frame was measured. Superimposed lines have been added by the author for clarity.

I think that while the dogs in the study were likely experiencing maximal carpal extension, **that degree of carpal extension is not out of the ordinary for dogs when cantering** (Figure 2). Instead of comparing the carpal extension angles of dog ascending the A-frame to those of dogs walking or even jumping, it might have been more relevant to compare the carpal angles of dogs ascending the A-frame to dogs that were cantering – the gait that is used when running agility.

The **dogs in the study** were running at an average of 6.7 meters per second, indicating that they **were cantering or galloping**. An examination of the literature of dogs that were trotting, which is a slower gait, demonstrated maximal carpal angles for Beagles of 49.2 degrees, for Rottweilers of 61.5 degrees, and for Labradors of 71.8

degrees. A search of the internet did not turn up studies of carpal angles of dogs cantering or galloping. However, slow-motion, high-resolution videos of Greyhounds galloping permitted measurement of maximal carpal angles from still photographs. **Dogs galloping on grass demonstrated carpal extension angles of about 64°** (Figure 2), slightly greater than those measured in the agility dogs going up the A-frame in this study. **The carpal angle of dogs ascending the A-frame, therefore, is no more than that which the dog experiences cantering around the whole course.**

Figure 2. The normal angle of carpal extension in a cantering dog is no different than that measured while ascending the A-frame in this study.

Having said that, many dogs approach the A-frame quickly and when they hit it, there can be tremendous concussion. Slowing the dog slightly prior to the A-frame or having the dog approach it at a more vertical angle might mitigate this concussion.

In any case, kudos to the authors of this study for addressing questions that are important to the health of our active dogs!

For references, see Notes, p. 138.

18. It's a Real Pain

"MAKE him do it!"

"He's just giving you the doggie dewclaw!"

"Pick him up and throw him over the jump!"

These were some of the comments I heard as I tried to understand why my experienced obedience dog would not jump the utility bar jump. This was a long time ago, but it is a lesson I have never forgotten.

Bannor, my beautiful Golden Retriever, was 9½ years old and we were just coming off a winter break, hoping to get the last 15 points we needed to complete his Obedience Trial Championship (OTCH).

We had spent a long, frustrating 3½ years garnering 85 OTCH points. Bannor was a great obedience dog, but in those days, points were not awarded unless you placed first or second in the class, and every weekend we found ourselves competing against the top 10 obedience dogs in the country. I swear I could drive into the parking lot and after checking out the cars that were there, know whether we'd get points or not that weekend.

That spring, whenever I set up the directed jumping exercise and signaled for Bannor to take the bar jump, he would run up to it and stop dead in his tracks. In those days, this 23-inch Golden Retriever had to jump a 34-inch bar jump! The weird thing was, if I walked over and tapped the bar, he would leap over the jump from a stand-still! Maybe that explained some of the comments made by bystanders at the training facility.

But I knew that this sweet boy didn't have an oppositional bone in his body. If he could have jumped over the moon for me, he would have. At about that time, I was starting to have a little trouble seeing things up close, a condition called presbyopia that most people begin to experience in middle age. I couldn't help wondering whether Bannor was having trouble with his eyesight, especially with focusing on objects up close. Perhaps the black and white stripes of the obedience bar jump added to his difficulty.

Even though Bannor had had clear ophthalmology examinations every year, I took him to an ophthalmologist and asked specifically about whether he might be having trouble focusing on close objects. The ophthalmologist confirmed my suspicions. Apparently the two of us were aging together! And that was the end of our OTCH campaign. I would not ask him to do something that he was physically unable to comply with.

The message that I wish to convey with this personal story is very simple: if you ever have a **training problem**, always consider first whether there might be a **physical reason**.

Every week in my veterinary practice, I see clients who for weeks, months, and regretfully, sometimes for years, have struggled with what they thought was a training problem, not recognizing that their dog was in pain. Perhaps the dog was missing weave pole entries, or struggled with the broad jump in obedience, or had just slowed down in field work, tracking, or any other sport. It seems our first thought is always to try to figure out how we can retrain the exercise. The dog did it before – why can't they do it now?

Well, it might just be because it hurts. If that's the case, then all the training in the world isn't going to change that and might just make it worse. And when my clients finally learn that their dog has an injury or some other physical problem, they experience extreme sadness and regret that they tried to fix something with training when it could only be fixed through healing.

If you ever have a training problem, always consider first whether there might be a physical reason.

We know that **most dogs won't show evidence of pain until it is moderate to severe**. If a dog was ever asked to describe its pain on a scale such as the 0-to-10 pain scale we are given at the ER, their scale would be 0-0-0-0-0-0-6-7-8-9-10. Many painful conditions such as back pain, soft tissue injuries of the shoulder, or iliopsoas strain can have very subtle or even absent clinical signs.

So, if you ever find yourself facing a knotty training problem, even if your dog's performance has just slowed a bit, or if you notice even a slightly reduced desire to play the game, stop training and immediately have your dog evaluated by a veterinarian.

Start with your general practitioner, who already knows your dog and who will likely initiate important blood and other tests to rule out a variety of systemic illnesses. If nothing obvious is found, **consider seeing a sports medicine or orthopedic**

specialist (they can be identified by the letters DACVSMR or DACVS, respectively, after their name) for further diagnostics to rule out a hidden musculoskeletal problem. That way you'll be sure you aren't asking your canine companion to do something that, while their heart is willing, their body is not able to do.

I was lucky to share my life with Bannor for another five years, and during that time we had many adventures that were much more fun than competing in obedience. I came to realize that in giving him the registered name Butterblac's Some Fools Dream, the universe had a different dream in mind.

We went for long hikes in the woods, we sat at the edge of a pond and contemplated the meaning of life (at least I did – I'm not sure what he was thinking, but I am sure they were deep canine thoughts), and we just spent time together, being present. Dogs are so good at that.

In memory of Can. Ch. Butterblac's Some Fools Dream Am. UD JH WCX; Can. WCI.

19. My Dog in Rehab Needs Stuff to Do

Ok, your canine buddy is on your team's injured reserve list. It's only temporary, but it's driving you and your teammate nuts! Your dog is used to being active – running, playing, wrestling with dog friends, and spending time training and competing with you in whatever games you play. **Your dog's brain thrives on stimulation!**

But now the veterinarian says you have to restrict your dog's activity. Phrases like "crate rest," "potty on leash only," and "no running or jumping" make you think that the next few weeks or months are going to be unbearable for both you and your active dog. You know that you must comply so that your dog can heal completely and get back to all those beloved games, but that's easier said than done.

Well, there's great news! **There are many things that you can do with a dog on restricted activity**, and they might, in fact, end up expanding, rather than contracting, your dog's repertoire of activities. Since dogs are highly intelligent beings, you can use this time to exercise their brains. You can also focus on exercises for the parts of their bodies that are not being rehabilitated.

> *There are many things you can do with a dog on restricted activity, and they might end up expanding, rather than contracting, your dog's repertoire of activities.*

Crate Rest
Let's deal with the 900-pound gorilla in the room first. Your veterinarian might have recommended crate rest, but long-term crate rest causes significant muscle atrophy. A day or two of strict crate rest after surgery might be necessary until your dog's body is cleared of anesthetic and the initial post-surgical pain is under control. Nonetheless, longer-term, significant confinement is needed for some conditions. So, clarify with your veterinarian what, exactly, they mean by crate rest, and ask about some of the following options.

Here are some alternatives that can keep your dog safely confined but still able to move around a little, change position and lie in various positions without risking injury:

- **An exercise pen** consisting of six or eight wire or plastic panels of an appropriate height (18 to 48 inches) clipped together and arranged in a circle is an ideal way to give your dog just a little more room. You can start by arranging the panels in a way that slightly expands your dog's space, and gradually increase the available area during the rehabilitation process. If your dog tries to climb or jump out of the pen, you can purchase or engineer a cover, which will keep all but the most insistent canine Houdini inside. If you place the pen in a well-frequented location, add favorite chew toys and a soft bed, and frequently throw food treats into the pen to reward your dog for settling down, it won't be long before your dog is thinking that this new living room fort is a pretty cool place to be.

- Another alternative is to have your dog restricted to a **small room**, such as a bathroom, as long as the flooring is non-slip. Instead of shutting the door, set up a see-through gate so that your dog can see what's going on and still feel like part of the family.

Pottying On Leash

Don't just clip on a 6-foot leash, go outside to the nearest grass, get the business done and go back inside. The outdoors offers a great deal of stimulation for all of your dog's senses. There are other dogs, people, food, trash, and other sights and scents much more interesting to dogs than to us out there in the world. There is also the sun, the rain, the breezes – so much to enjoy. Let your dog experience these things while safely on leash.

Make potty time a positive experience. Sure, you might need to start with your dog on a 6-foot leash but, depending on your dog and the stage of rehabilitation, you might be able to gradually increase its length. Take your dog to the most scent-worthy places in your yard or the neighborhood and let him or her just settle down or even wander around, taking in the environment. If it's okay with your veterinarian, maybe a roll in the freshly mowed grass is called for. Personally, I think that a few grass stains are a colorful addition to most dogs' coats, especially if it means better emotional health (Figure 1).

Figure 1. Most dogs love to roll. This dog uses a ball as a back scratcher.

Exercising Your Dog's Brain

Have you ever taken a class in which you struggled so hard to figure something out that afterwards you felt mentally exhausted and needed a nap? For me, it would be physics. Well, dogs experience the same thing; mental exercise can give you a lot more bang for your buck than physical exercise when it comes to tiring your injured dog out. Here are several games that will help your dog settle down and sleep soundly. I bet you can think of others as well!

1. Puzzle Games

There are dozens of games on the market that are designed so that your dog must solve a puzzle to get a piece of food. Some are very simple toys that require the dog to move an object into a certain position before the food will drop out. Others require your dog to initiate a series of complex moves such as moving sliders and opening drawers before the food is presented (Figure 2). Experiment with them, starting with the simpler ones, and seeing how far your brilliant dog can advance. You may need to make them easy at first to help your dog stay motivated, but over time you can up the ante as your dog's problem-solving skills improve.

2. Food Activities

Give your dog a marrow bone with a little meat still on the outside. That can make a dog happy for an hour or more, chewing all the gristle off the outside and digging out the marrow. If your dog is not used to fresh, fatty foods, you might limit his or her time with the bone initially to be sure that their gastrointestinal tract is up to the task. Keep in mind that there is a risk of tooth fracture when dogs chew hard objects such as bones, so another option is a bully stick or other edible rawhide. To reduce any choking risk, chews should only be given while supervised and removed when they are small enough that your dog could swallow them.

You might also fill a Kong™ or other similar toy with your dog's food, sealing it with xylitol-free peanut butter or yogurt. Freezing this treat will make it last even longer. There are dozens of good recipes for fillings on the internet, as well as websites that have suggestions for homemade food-dispensing toys.

Figure 2. Puzzle toys can occupy dogs for hours.

Teach your dog to catch food. This usually requires minimal movement by your dog if you start by tossing the food from a very short distance and gradually move farther away. Use foods of different weights, for example, kibble vs popcorn, so that your dog learns to really track the food, regardless of its speed.

3. Scent Games
These can be played inside and outside, giving your dog lots of different experiences.
a. *Find the Cookie!* Hide some (preferably smelly) food treats in your house. Start in a small room to begin with but expand the area as your dog gets better and can move around more. Initially just place the treats in obvious locations on the floor. As your dog's scenting skills sharpen, start putting them under sofa cushions, in corners where there are heating/cooling registers that swirl the scent around, and under a crumpled blanket so that your dog needs to dig for that buried treasure. One warning, though, don't hide treats on counters or kitchen tables if you don't want your dog to learn to counter surf!

Figure 3. The shell game.

b. *The Shell Game.* Hide a very smelly treat under one of three plastic containers and encourage your dog to identify its location (Figure 3). Then gradually start using foods with less scent. Hint: High fat, high protein foods have more odor than high carbohydrate foods.

Remember to watch your dog's weight while using these games. If possible, use food that is part of your dog's daily ration. Or use foods with higher levels of proteins and fats, such as microwaved hot dog, bacon, or other meat slices, rather than store-bought treats that are often high in carbohydrates. If your dog is on a diet, use low-calorie treats like baby carrots or apples, in addition to the more delicious ones. You can place the low-calorie treats into a baggie with some fatty treats and shake them around to coat the lower value treats with scent to increase their appeal.

4. Train Some Tricks
There are lots of tricks that involve minimal movement. Most of these require just a little understanding of reward-based learning on your part. Figure out a way to get your dog to perform the desired behavior (this might require several steps to progressively approximate the final action), and the instant your dog performs the desired behavior praise and give a treat. Don't add a verbal cue to perform the exercise until your dog is performing the final behavior. The best games are ones that play off something your dog already loves to do. So, watch your dog and turn his joy into tricks!

Easy Tricks to Try

Here are a few examples of easy tricks, but you'll be able to think of lots more!

a. Stick Out Your Tongue. You can teach your dog to stick out her tongue by holding a treat in front of her nose and clicking or praising as soon as her tongue comes out to lick the treat. Another way to get a dog to stick its tongue out is to blow in her face. Once your dog is regularly sticking her tongue out, add a verbal cue like, "What do you think of rehab?"

b. Hug Something. Teach your dog to touch its nose to a small, approximately 1-inch diameter piece of paper glued to a wooden spoon by praising and treating as his face gets gradually closer to the spoon. Make sure your dog's nose touches the paper, not the spoon. Then transfer the paper to your cheek, so that your dog snuggles his nose up against you (Figure 4).

c. Put Away Your Toys. Hasn't everyone wished that their dogs would put away their toys? This one is easy – just teach your dog to pick up whatever you point at and put it in a box. Once you put a verbal cue on this behavior, your dog will start putting away his toys without you needing to point at them.

d. Help Around the House. As your dog is able to do more, you can teach a variety of useful tricks such as finding the TV remote, how to bump cabinets closed, and to open or close the refrigerator. Just make sure she can't open it when you're not around or your grocery bill may increase exponentially, along with your dog's waistline!

e. Name That Toy. First teach your dog to pick up a toy when you give it a name. As a reward, play with that toy together. Then add another toy and give it another name. When your dog picks up that one in response to its name, play with that one. Then try alternating names so that your dog only gets to play when they choose the correct toy. Add more toys *ad infinitum*.

f. Sports Shorts. There are lots of components of your favorite sports that don't require a lot of movement. For example, many of the Rally moves and the Obedience scent discrimination exercise are appropriate for dogs undergoing rehabilitation therapy. For agility dogs, you can teach right and left turns, come to your left and right sides, and other ground work that doesn't involve running.

Figure 4. Helix's version of Hug Something.

Exercise Your Dog's Body

When your dog's injury is localized to one area of the body, there's no reason not to keep the other parts of the body fit. That will help your dog recover from the injury more quickly and will help prevent compensatory injuries.

1. Grow a Few Muscles

If your dog has injured its elbow, you can safely use targeted exercises to strengthen the rear legs. Conversely, if your dog has a hip injury, there's no reason not to build your dog's shoulder muscles. There are many ways to safely strengthen a dog's muscles. The best strengthening exercises have the following characteristics: they are non-impact, they are targeted to specific areas of the body, and they involve working to overload. That's great news, because it means that most of these exercises can be performed in the comfort of your own living room.

Examples:

a. Front Limb Injuries. Improve your dog's core muscles by teaching him or her to sit up on their haunches (yes, studies show this is completely safe; See Chapter 4). Alternatively, have your dog move from a sit to a stand and back to a sit repeatedly without moving the front feet. Strengthen the rear by having your dog reach to touch a target placed behind or beside them on the ground or at various elevations.*

b. Rear limb injuries. Teach your dog to wave with their front paw higher than their head (Figure 5) or give you a high-9 (like a high-5 but placing the paw in any of nine different positions in front of the body).*

Figure 5. Alba demonstrates The Wave.

*A flash drive with videos demonstrating these exercises and many more can be purchased here: https://caninesports.com/product/ffl-videos/ or videos can be live streamed individually here: https://vimeo.com/ondemand/caninefitforlife

2. Make Walks More Fun

Going for a walk with your dog shouldn't be like going on the Bataan Death March. Many rehabilitation professionals prescribe gradually increasing lengths of walks. Clients who are serious about their dogs' rehabilitation often take their dogs out day after day for walks along the sidewalk or streets in their neighborhood, checking to make sure that they have spent the prescribed amount of time on the walk. In addition, since walking in the same places day after day can be boring, they often just stick in those earphones and listen to music, podcasts, or books on tape, paying little attention to their canine companion.

Even at the best of times, walks are not a particularly good form of exercise for most dogs. They are relatively high-impact, they do not target the specific part of the body that needs the exercise, and it's very hard to know when your dog has had too much or not enough (see Chapter 11).

Figure 6. Quality time one-on-one.

Rather than a period of rehabilitation being a time of reduced activity, you can make this a time filled with new activities and a renewed relationship.

Instead, view going for a walk as a Good for the Soul exercise (Figure 6). Not just your dog's soul, but yours, too. Here's what to do. Put your dog on a long line of 12 to 20 feet. Think of a place where you can go that is new and preferably in the middle of nature. A park, or a path in the woods, or a public garden where on-leash dogs are allowed are all great places. Even your and possibly your neighbors' front yards will do in a pinch. Take your dog out and let him or her sniff and pee, and poop, and sniff some more to their heart's content. Don't rush it. Don't time it. Just be. And while you're at it, breathe. Deeply. Be present and enjoy where you are, spending quality time with that amazing creature that you love and are helping to heal.

For references, see Notes, p. 138.

20. The Genetics of Athletic Success

Dogs are the most physically varied species on earth, having been selected for many different functions - you've surely heard the adage "form follows function."

A fascinating study compared whole-genome DNA sequence data between sport-hunting and terrier breeds, groups thought to be at the ends of a continuum in both form and function, as well as in a number of other breeds of dogs.

The goal of the study was to identify genes/gene groups that might underlie functions important for athletic ability.

Genes/Gene Groups Involved in Performance and Behavior

1. A total of 59 genes were strongly selected for in sport-hunting breeds (they examined spaniels, setters and pointers, but not retrievers). Those **genes are responsible for muscle, cardiovascular, and neurological functions**, which play such an important role in athleticism.

2. Sport-hunting dogs had a higher level of mutations in the genes *CDH23* and *MSRB3* as compared to terriers. Mutations in these **genes are linked to sensory impairment.** Interestingly, sport-hunting dogs are considered to be a less noise-sensitive group (because of the need to ignore gun shots) than terriers.

3. An examination of more than 1,000 agility dogs representing 100+ breeds showed that a specific allele of the **ROBO1 gene was associated with greater success in USDAA agility**. *ROBO1* encodes a brain protein that guides axons during development, and variations in this gene may result in variable cognitive plasticity. This gene might affect the ability to identify and acquire environmental information so that task-specific responses can be executed during the sport of agility.

Dario Egidi

4. An allele of *TRPM3* (which functions in vascular smooth muscle contraction) was significantly **associated with increased racing speed in Whippets** (but not Greyhounds), accounting for 11.6% of the total variance in racing performance.

5. The gene *RSPO2*, which had been shown to be **associated with furnishings** (mustache and eyebrows) was selected for in terriers, as were the *SHANK2* and *ORX1* genes, which are **involved in hyperactivity and panic responses**.

This study provides strong evidence that various breeds of dogs have been selected for genetically improved endurance, cardiac function, blood flow, and cognitive performance, all of which can affect athletic ability.

What relevance does this study have to you? Well, this study suggests that if you are interested in success in athletic competition, you might tip the balance in your favor if you select your next teammate from lines of dogs that have been bred specifically for success in those competitions.

As we learn more about the genetics of dogs, will we eventually identify the 'champion genome?'

For references, see Notes, p. 138.

21. Telomeres and Your Dog's Lifespan

A collaborative study by researchers in Canada and the US showed that **dogs with longer telomeres live longer**. What are telomeres, you ask? Telomeres are caps at the end of each strand of DNA that protect your dog's chromosomes, like aglets, the plastic tips at the end of shoelaces. Without aglets, shoelaces become frayed so they can no longer do their job. Likewise, without telomeres, DNA strands become damaged, and your dog's cells can't function correctly.

Dogs with shorter telomeres have a shorter lifespan. However, we can lengthen our dog's telomeres by providing good nutrition and exercise.

Cells must divide for our dogs to remain healthy. The problem is, **every time a cell divides, a piece of the telomere is cut off**. That is why cells eventually die after replicating many times. **Anything that causes a cell to divide more often will increase the rate of aging of that cell.** And of course, when cells age, so does the dog that is made up of those cells.

In this study, the researchers measured the length of telomeres in peripheral blood cells from 175 different dogs of 15 different breeds (**Figure 1**). They then graphed the telomere lengths against mortality data from a meta-analysis of 74,556 dogs. They found that **telomere length was a strong predictor of average life span**. This finding had a p value of < 0.0001 which means that there is a one in ten thousand chance that the results were not just due to chance.

Interestingly, the study also showed that **dogs lose telomere DNA 10 times faster than humans do**, which is consistent with the fact that dogs live about 1/10th as long as people do. They also determined that **male dogs lose telomere length slightly faster than females**, which is also true in humans. Note, however, that this study showed correlation, not causation. The causation could be due to other factors, such as breed size, which also has been correlated with breed life span.

In fact, **the correlation between breed size and life span could be related to telomere length**. If you think about it, an Irish Wolfhound, which weighs about 23 oz at

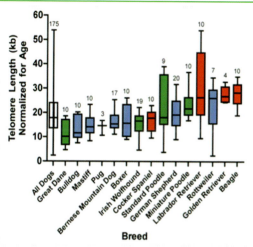

Figure 1. Telomere lengths of 15 breeds. Dogs were categorized into working (blue), herding (green), and hunting (red) breeds. The line in the middle of each colored bar represents the median number of telomeres for that breed. The horizontal lines at the top and the bottom of each vertical line represent the maximum and minimum number of telomeres for that breed. The colored bar represents the telomere lengths for the middle 50% of dogs.

birth and about 160 lb as an adult, multiplies its weight approximately 112 times to reach adult size. That means that those cells are undergoing many rounds of cell division, cutting off pieces of the telomeres each time, just to reach adulthood.

In contrast, a Yorkshire Terrier weighs on average four oz at birth and seven lb as an adult, which means that it multiplies its birthweight by only 26 times to reach adulthood. Theoretically, **the smaller dog would therefore retain its telomere length longer, and thus live longer.**

Further, the study demonstrated that **breeds with shorter mean telomere lengths have an increased probability of death from cardiovascular, respiratory, gastrointestinal, and muscle disease**. This makes sense, because those tissues have a very high rate of cell division. In contrast, breeds with long mean telomere length were more likely to die of neurological conditions, which also makes sense because neurological tissue doesn't replicate very quickly at all.

The Body's Reversal System
Countering the fact that telomeres get shorter and shorter over time is the fact that **the body produces an enzyme called telomerase, which can lengthen telomeres,** reversing the effect of natural aging on the DNA strands. **Telomerase activity is very high in cancer cells**, providing one mechanism by which these cells replicate continuously and do not become senescent. That is consistent with the fact that in this study, telomere length did not correlate with the rates of cancer in the various breeds.

The good news is that **we may be able to lengthen our dog's telomeres through the care we give**. Regular **physical activity**, a diet rich in **fresh food** and **antioxidants** (check out Chapters 24 & 25 on how, exactly, to do that), and **low stress** have all been shown to increase telomere length in multiple species, including dogs and people. That is such great news, because it gives us some control over our dogs' longevity.

There is one last point about telomeres that is important to note. Telomere length increases with the age of the male dog producing the sperm. At least in humans, **offspring conceived by older fathers have longer telomeres than those conceived by younger fathers**. If this relationship holds true in dogs, as suggested by their similar telomere biology, it might be **possible to significantly increase the average healthy life span of our dogs by using sperm from older males**, over just a few generations. Some breeders are already doing that in an attempt to increase the longevity of the dogs they produce, which is pretty cool!

For references, see Notes, p. 138.

22. No Weigh!

It is important to maintain your active dog at a correct weight. **People** who are overweight have an **increased risk of cancer** and **other systemic diseases** as well as **early death**, and one study indicates that dogs kept at a normal weight can live up to 2½ years longer than overweight dogs (Chapter 23). Keeping a dog in optimal to slightly lean body condition has been shown to **decrease the risk of osteoarthritis** a condition with which many older dogs suffer.

Purina and Royal Canin have proposed 9- and 5-point body condition scores that use visual and descriptive methods to assess weight, but I have a better method.

Problems with Visual Body Condition Scoring:

1. Visual body condition scoring systems might apply to a short-coated, average-structured dog, but **what about dogs with big barrel chests and heavy, wavy, or sculpted coats**, such as the Bernese Mountain Dog or the Portuguese Water Dog?

2. When the scoring system says for a score of 5: "ribs palpable without excess fat covering," how do we define "excess?"

3. Purina's own study showed that a dog with a BCS of 5 out of 9 could have a percent body fat between 13 and 22%. That range is so broad that **I don't feel that the BCS method is specific enough** to help keep our dogs at a healthy weight.

Weigh your Dog?

Putting your dog on a scale to monitor weight can be problematic as well. Many dogs are **too big to hold while you try to weigh both yourself and the dog**, then subtract your own weight. Most home scales are **not sensitive enough to accurately weigh dogs under about 25 lb (11 kg).** In any case, there is **no specific weight** for any given dog, since they vary so much in size, bone, and muscle. If you ask a veterinarian to tell you how many pounds or kilograms your dog needs to lose, they are just making a wild guess (many veterinarians have confirmed this for me).

There's a better way! Just feel the thickness of your dog's subcutaneous fat using the **Tissue Tent Test**. This is easily done over the last three to four ribs, about 1/3 of the way down from the topline (Figure 1). In that area, there is just a layer of skin and a layer of subcutaneous fat overlying the ribs. Here's how to feel that layer of fat.

The Tissue Tent Test

With your thumb and index finger, press in deeply towards the ribs and then, while continuing to press inward, close your thumb and index finger together, **pinching all of the tissue between your fingers**. With the tissue gathered between your fingers, stop for a second, then **pull slowly outward while still gripping, making a tent** of your dog's tissue. You will (usually very quickly) feel a layer of slightly bumpy-textured tissue below the skin slip through your fingers in the direction of the red arrow in Figure 2. That's your dog's layer of subcutaneous fat. Feel it a few times until you can estimate its thickness. In a fit dog, that layer should be as thin as a folded piece of duct tape.

Many people can't feel that layer at first. Often, it's because they are doing everything too fast. Remember: **pinch deeply, stop, grip tightly** as you pull the tissue tent together, **stop again**, then **slowly and gently pull** the tent away from the skin, and you'll soon feel it.

Use the Tissue Tent Test to monitor your dog's body fat layer weekly and adjust your dog's food intake until it is at the correct thickness. It's as easy as that!

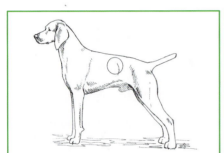

Figure 1. To feel the layer of subcutaneous fat, pinch the tissues in the area of the last few ribs (circle). In that area, there is just skin and subcutaneous fat overlying the ribs.

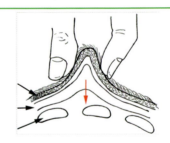

Figure 2. When the mobile skin and subcutaneous tissues over the ribcage are pinched and pulled away from the ribs, the layer of subcutaneous fat is the first to slip through the fingers in the direction of the red arrow.

For references, see Notes, p. 139.

23. How to Make Your Dog Live Longer. It's Easy!

As my dog grows older, I often look at his greying face and hope I will have him for many more years. And when it becomes obvious that I will have to say goodbye to one of my dogs, I always wish that we could have just a few more days together. I'm sure you have felt that way too.

That's one wish that you can make come true! **You can easily increase your dog's life span by up to two years and it won't cost you a thing**. In fact, it will save you money! Too good to be true?

Fit dog   Fat dog

You can easily increase your dog's life span by up to two years and it won't cost you a thing.

In 2019, a group of scientists published a study that looked at the **lifespans of over 50,000 dogs of 12 different breeds** living in North America. That's a LOT of dogs! They asked a very simple question. What is the expected lifespan of dogs that are overweight when they visit a veterinary hospital in middle age (between 6½ and 8½ years) as compared to dogs that are of normal weight?

The authors defined overweight as being a 4 or 5 on a body condition scale of 1 to 5. Normal weight dogs were a 3 on that scale. The 5-point scale represented dogs that were described by veterinarians on visual examination and palpation as being very thin - 1, thin - 2, normal - 3, overweight - 4, or markedly obese - 5. Dogs in both the overweight and normal categories were then matched by breed, sex, visit age, visit year, latitude and longitude, and spay and neuter status.

It is well documented that dogs that have had their ovaries or testicles removed have a lower metabolic rate and tend to gain weight unless their food intake is reduced. Thus, it was important for the study to ensure that intact dogs were not compared with spayed or neutered dogs. After examining the data, sexually intact dogs were removed from the study because there were too few of them in the dataset. This statement is certainly a concern for the future of pet dogs, but that is an entirely different topic. Nonetheless, this study only examined lifespans of spayed or neutered dogs.

For all 12 breeds of dogs selected for the study, **the median age at death for overweight dogs was significantly less than for dogs of normal body condition**. These data are summarized in the table below. The estimated reduction in median life span for the overweight group relative to the normal weight group ranged from five months for male German Shepherd Dogs, to two and a half years for male Yorkshire Terriers. Although the authors looked at only 12 breeds, the consistent finding that overweight dogs had shorter lifespans suggests that this effect is likely to be present in every breed.

Mean Differences in Age at Death for Dogs of Different Breeds and Sizes

Breed Size	Neutered Males Median Life Span (years)			Spayed Females Median Life Span (years)		
	Normal Weight	Overweight	Difference	Normal Weight	Overweight	Difference
Chihuahua	16.0	13.9	2.1	16.1	14.0	2.1
Pomeranian	15.5	13.7	1.8	15.5	13.6	1.9
Yorkshire Terrier	16.2	13.7	2.5	15.5	13.5	2.0
Shih Tzu	14.5	13.8	0.7	14.5	13.9	0.6
Dachshund	16.4	14.1	2.3	16.4	14.1	2.3
Avg Small Dog	**15.7**	**13.8**	**1.9**	**15.6**	**13.8**	**1.8**
American Cocker Spaniel	14.9	13.4	1.5	14.8	13.3	1.5
Beagle	15.2	13.2	2.0	15.3	13.3	2.0
Pit Bull	13.8	13.0	0.8	13.8	12.9	0.9
Avg Medium Dog	**14.6**	**13.2**	**1.4**	**14.6**	**13.2**	**1.4**
Boxer	12.4	11.8	0.6	12.3	11.7	0.6
German Shepherd Dog	12.5	12.1	0.4	13.1	12.5	0.6
Golden Retriever	13.3	12.5	0.8	13.5	12.7	0.8
Labrador Retriever	13.3	12.7	0.6	13.6	13.0	0.6
Avg Large Dog	**12.9**	**12.3**	**0.6**	**13.1**	**12.5**	**0.6**

This study's results are consistent with a previous one examining lifespan in a colony of overweight vs normal weight Labrador Retrievers. However, this is the first study to examine such a large number of dogs living in family environments from a large number of popular breeds (an average of more than 3,800 dogs of each breed).

Interestingly, the difference in lifespan between overweight and normal weight dogs was greatest for small and medium-sized dogs and less for dogs of the larger breeds. This might be explained by the demonstrated increased prevalence of fatal cancers in spayed and neutered large breed dogs. A review of these data can be found at: https://caninesports.com/wp-content/uploads/2021/05/CSP-Gonadectomy-Rethinking.pdf

Discovering the Dog
How To Make Your Dog Live Longer

The increased prevalence of cancer in spayed or neutered large-breed dogs might have negated the effect of good body condition in these breeds. Because intact large breed dogs don't experience this increased cancer effect, their median lifespans might, in fact, be longer than those of spayed or neutered dogs. That would have to be confirmed in another study that included intact dogs.

Dogs that are overweight are more susceptible to a variety of chronic conditions including osteoarthritis and other orthopedic diseases, diabetes, cancer, respiratory, cardiovascular, and renal disease as well as a reduced quality of life. In fact, in a recent review, **the financial impact of having an obese dog was estimated to be approximately $2000 a year**! That and the reduced annual cost of dog food for a normal-weight dog as compared to an overweight one provides significant financial incentives (in addition to the clear lifespan incentive) to keep our dogs at a normal weight.

One last point. Although it is tempting to do so, we cannot assume that the median survival ages noted in these studies are typical for these breeds. That's because this study only included dogs that had not died before 9½ years of age and that continued to be cared for in the veterinary practices from which the data were obtained. That was the only way the authors could ensure accurate data. Since many dogs, unfortunately, die before 9½ years of age, these data show artificially extended life spans. Darn it! I sure would have loved it if the median life span of a Golden Retriever was 13.3 to 13.5 years!

Still, **the great news about this study is that we do have some control over how long our dogs live.** By keeping our dogs at a normal weight throughout their lives, we can stack the longevity cards in our dogs' favor. Then, when the day comes that we know it is time to say goodbye, we can take solace in the fact that our dogs are likely much older than they would have been if they had been overweight. And that's great news!

The financial impact of having an obese dog was estimated to be approximately $2000 per year.

A well-muscled dog of correct weight.

For references, see Notes, p. 139.

24. Inflammatory Food?
Co-authored by Donna Raditic DVM, DACVIM (Nutrition)*

Fifty years ago, the sugar industry quietly paid researchers at Harvard University to indicate that dietary fat was the major nutritional cause of heart disease. Their study was published in the prominent New England Journal of Medicine, and it laid the foundation for **decades of nutrition misinformation perpetrated on the public** by well-meaning organizations such as the American Heart Association.

Given that there are only three major components of nutrition – fat, carbohydrates, and protein, of which protein is the most costly – it was inevitable that the emphasis on low-fat diets would lead to greater consumption of sugar. This was a big score for the sugar industry, but not so much for us. We now know that diets high in refined grains and added sugars have numerous detrimental effects on our metabolism, leading to adverse lipid profiles, and contributing to obesity, diabetes, cardiovascular disease, and cancer.

For a fascinating, detailed history of the food industry's sabotage of human health in the name of profit, I recommend reading *Metabolical* by Robert H Lustig MD MSL.

Dog Food Facts

Dog afficionado that I am, my thoughts then turned to whether high levels of readily digested carbohydrates might also be a problem for dogs, particularly given that dogs have a carnivorous bias nutritionally. Here's what I learned:

Fact: Most dogs in North America (estimates suggest 80% to 90%) are fed kibble.

Fact: On average, kibble contains between 46% and 74% carbohydrates.

Fact: Percent carbohydrates required by adult dogs to sustain life: zero.

---

*Dr. Donna Raditic is a Board-Certified Veterinary Nutritionist. As a founder of Nutrition and Integrative Medicine Consultants, she provides education and consulting on companion animal nutrition and integrative care. She is also cofounder of the not-for-profit, Companion Animal Nutrition and Wellness Institute that works to fund nutrition education programs and independent nutrition research.

These facts suggest that it is critically important to understand the make-up of kibble dog foods, which contain more carbohydrates than either fat or protein, to be sure that they promote health and longevity for our dogs. As you'll see, however, it's not the carbohydrates that are the problem, but how those carbohydrates are processed during the manufacture of kibble.

How Kibble is Made

All kibbles are made in essentially the same way. Wet and dry food ingredients, some of which already have gone through heating and other processing, are mixed to form a dough. High pressure and heat are applied to cook the dough which is then forced through tubes. Pieces of the extruded tube-shaped dough are cut off to make pellets. The pellets are then passed through a heated dryer to remove any remaining moisture. Finally, the food is sprayed with animal fats to improve flavor, vitamins to attempt to replace those damaged during the heating process, artificial colors to improve visual appeal, and preservatives. That's how it's done. Kill off some of the nutrients, then spray them back on. Interestingly, this is the same multi-step food processing method, termed 'ultra-processing,' that is used to produce our ready-to-eat-breakfast cereals!

The Maillard Reaction and AGEs (The Whaaat?)

It turns out that the superheating process during the production of kibble changes the quality of some nutrients in a way that no spray can replace. When certain amino acids within a protein are heated in the presence of sugars, a series of chemical rearrangements occurs, called the Maillard reaction. The final products of this reaction are called advanced glycation end-products, or AGEs. This process is irreversible, and it, in fact, decreases the availability of certain amino acids in the dog's food, because they become bound up as part of the AGEs.

You Are What You Eat

These AGEs are absorbed in the gut and enter the circulation, where they are distributed to all parts of the body. Because AGEs are big and bulky, they are resistant to degradation, so **they accumulate and gradually become part of the protein structure of the entire body**. Studies are beginning to demonstrate the **numerous effects these AGE-modified proteins have on health and disease** in both humans and our canine companions.

Here are some of the known effects of AGEs (Figure 1):
- AGEs stimulate inflammatory responses, creating a state of **chronic systemic inflammation**, which is associated with the development of **cancers** in both humans and dogs.
- AGEs can hinder the **repair** of tissues, especially tissues that have a high protein content, such as ligaments and tendons. This, in turn, can lead to more rapid signs of **aging**.
- AGEs in humans have been linked to atherosclerosis, kidney disease, retinopathy, osteoarthritis, neurodegenerative diseases, and diabetes mellitus.
- Increased levels of AGEs in dogs have been detected in tissues of animals with **diabetes, cataracts, osteoarthritis, canine cognitive dysfunction syndrome, vascular dysfunction**, and **atherosclerosis**.
- The immune system interacts with AGEs resulting in increased production of inflammatory cytokines. This can lead to an increase in allergic responses in the gut, expressed as **inflammatory bowel disease**.

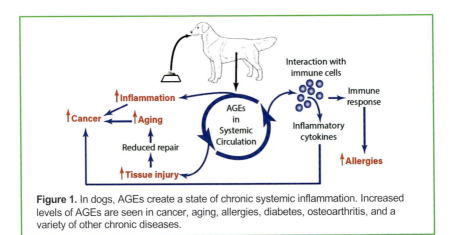

Figure 1. In dogs, AGEs create a state of chronic systemic inflammation. Increased levels of AGEs are seen in cancer, aging, allergies, diabetes, osteoarthritis, and a variety of other chronic diseases.

The content of AGEs in processed commercial pet foods is about the same as in processed human foods products. In pet foods, **AGE levels in canned food are higher than kibble** which, in turn, are higher than a fresh, minimally processed food. However, **the average daily intake of AGEs by most dogs is 122 times higher than that of humans** (as a percentage of metabolic body weight)! This is exacerbated by the fact most dogs eat exclusively ultra-processed food for most of their lives!

Taken together, these data suggest that **by reducing our dogs' exposure to dietary AGEs we might improve their overall health and longevity**.

What Can You Do?
Once we learned that heating protein with sugars at high temperatures results in the production of AGEs, and that AGEs contribute to chronic diseases, cancer, and aging in dogs, we decided to reduce the exposure of our own dogs to AGEs. For us, that

translates to **feeding a diet that contains as high a percentage of fresh food as possible (Figure 2)** and **reducing the amount of kibble and canned food that our dogs consume**. Human nutritionists tell us to limit our grocery shopping as much as possible to items along the outside walls of the grocery store. That is where the freshest, least processed foods are found. We try to do the equivalent for our dogs.

I know you'd like us to name the specific dog foods we feed. But what's best for our dogs might not be best for yours. So, you're going to have to do some research. It's not that different from learning about which are the healthiest foods for your and your family. After all, would you spend your entire life eating just one, highly processed food at every meal?

Guidelines for Choosing the Best Dog Foods

- Choose foods that are sourced and processed in North America
- Rotate your dogs' foods among several select manufacturers to provide food from a variety of sources and using a variety of recipes. This helps reduce the effects of any unintended ingredient errors.
- Choose a food that has been formulated by qualified PhD or American College of Veterinary Nutrition (ACVN) nutritionists and put through feeding trials.
- Purchase minimally processed dog foods (commercial raw, cooked, or freeze-dried) – whatever makes you comfortable (Figure 2). Note that raw and cooked foods have similar digestibility.

Where can you find independent information to help you select the best food for your furry friend? While there is currently no gold-standard source for independent evaluation of dog foods, the Whole Dog Journal is a good start, with monthly issues devoted to reviewing the various forms of dog food. Luckily, there is an increasing number of fresh dog foods available on the market, even at the major pet food chains.

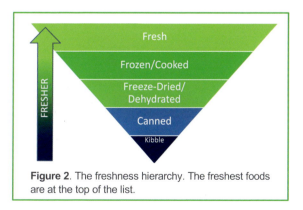

Figure 2. The freshness hierarchy. The freshest foods are at the top of the list.

It is not our intent to make you feel guilty for feeding kibble. We both fed kibble for many years, and still use it for training treats and when traveling. Kibble is convenient and less expensive than fresh foods. Many dogs have done well on kibble diets for decades. But after learning of the detrimental effects of the products of heat-processed foods on canine metabolism, we decided to try doing just a little better.

We strongly believe that **most dogs will benefit from the replacement of at least some portion of their highly processed foods with a fresher alternative**. Certainly, the evidence suggests that for dogs with allergies, chronic osteoarthritis, diabetes, or other chronic diseases, replacing highly processed food with a fresher alternative is likely to improve their health and longevity. Why not give it a try?

For references, see Notes, p. 140.

25. Smart Supplementation
Co-authored by Donna Raditic DVM, DACVIM (Nutrition)*

There are thousands of canine dietary supplements out there, and every company is vying for your attention and your money. Their advertisements show action photos of world-class canine athletes and use terminology that suggest that their supplement will magically provide your dog with health, vitality, longevity, and peak performance.

If you are reading this, you know that's just not true. But should you provide your dog with supplements at all? And if so, which ones, how much, and how often? Let's look at the scientific evidence.

Supplement Suggestions

1. Providing a supplement means that you believe that **your dog is not getting sufficient amounts** of that component in its daily diet. Vitamins and minerals in their natural, fresh forms often have better bioavailability and retention in tissues than their synthetic counterparts. So, we know that we first need to begin with a healthy fresh (minimally processed) diet (see Chapter 24).

2. Next, ask yourself: What is the **scientific evidence** that my dog should be getting this supplement? See list of recommended supplements and the scientific evidence below.

3. Many supplements have a mixture of components so that the manufacturer can claim their supplement as unique. Do you really **need all those components**? Remember, each additional additive reduces the amounts of some of the others, so that the supplement remains a reasonable size for the dog to ingest. So, make sure that each ingredient you give counts!

4. Stack the deck in your favor – only buy supplements from manufacturers that: (a) **provide data on all the supplement's active and inactive ingredients** in the packaging, (b) are **established** and have a **reputation** to uphold, and (c) are a **member of the National Animal Supplement Council (NASC)**.

5. Purchase supplements **designed for and tested in dogs**. Supplements designed for humans might not have the same bioavailability as those for dogs and some might even have ingredients, such as xylitol, that are unsafe or even fatal for dogs.

> Ask yourself, "What is the scientific evidence that my dog should be getting this supplement?"

---

*Dr. Donna Raditic is a Board-Certified Veterinary Nutritionist. As a founder of Nutrition and Integrative Medicine Consultants, she provides education and consulting on companion animal nutrition and integrative care. She is also cofounder of the not-for-profit, Companion Animal Nutrition and Wellness Institute that works to fund nutrition education programs and independent nutrition research.

Recommended Supplements for Healthy Active Dogs (and the Evidence)

- *Omega-3 Fatty Acids* – Of all the available canine supplements, the evidence for adding omega-3 fatty acids to the diet is the strongest. We recommend feeding 50 - 100 mg/kg of the exact omega-3 fatty acids called docosahexaenoic acid (DHA) and eicosapentaenoic acid (EPA) daily. These omega-3 fatty acids are found in oils from animal sources such as wild fish oil and algae oil, but not in flax or other plant-based oils. Make sure the product you use has been tested for heavy metals and toxins.

  The Scientific Evidence: Two meta-studies concluded that there is strong evidence for the systemic anti-inflammatory effects of omega-3 fatty acid supplementation.

- *Probiotics* – Probiotics are defined by the World Health Organization (WHO) as live microorganisms which, when administered in adequate amounts, confer a health benefit on the host. Be sure to use a product designed for or tested on dogs.

  The Scientific Evidence: Probiotics can reduce the severity of canine allergies, improve inflammatory bowel disease, and boost responses to vaccines.

- *Joint-Protective Nutraceuticals* – We recommend a dose of about 15-30 mg/kg of a glucosamine/chondroitin per day. Dosing is usually based of the chondroitin component (i.e., mg of chondroitin per serving). Many products contain other anti-inflammatory components such as avocado-soybean unsaponifiables (ASU) or *Boswellia* and these can be helpful as long as their presence doesn't reduce the dose of the main ingredient's glucosamine and chondroitin. We do not recommend giving oral glucosamine/chondroitin joint supplements if your dog is prescribed injectable veterinary glycosaminoglycan products such as Adequan.

  The Scientific Evidence: The evidence for this supplement is weaker than for omega-3 fatty acids. A meta-analysis of a variety of dietary supplements for osteoarthritis in humans suggested improvement of pain and function with glucosamine, chondroitin, MSM, and ASU, although they stated that there was also a need for higher quality evidence.

- *Antioxidants* – Antioxidants are thought to be most effective if fed in their natural form. Blueberries are very high in antioxidants as are some other fruits and vegetables.

Marek Kosmal

The Scientific Evidence: Studies show that diets containing antioxidants improve cognitive function in old dogs. A study of bladder cancer suggested an intake of vegetables may prevent or slow progression of cancer in dogs.

- **Amino acids** – Many dog foods, particularly kibbles, provide the majority of their amino acids from plant sources, since these are cheaper. **Dogs need certain essential amino acids and other nutrients that can only come from animal sources**. We recommend adding amino acids to the diet of dogs being fed kibble or canned food to ensure that they receive an abundance of the correct, animal-sourced amino acids.

  In dogs that are fed exclusively kibble, selective amino acids can be bound up into large, poorly digested molecules called advanced glycation end products called AGEs (Chapter 24). One example of an amino acid supplement, ProBalance (AVN), has been designed by an independent, board-certified veterinary nutritionist to supply all the essential, animal-sourced amino acids and building blocks for important nutrients in a readily absorbable form.

There are other supplements that might be appropriate in dogs with certain diseases or injuries, but the above supplements are what we recommend for most healthy, active dogs.

For references, see Notes, p. 141.

26. Yeast - Yuck!

Figure 1. What's that brown stain around this dog's mouth? Yeast!

We have all seen dogs that have reddish-brown tear stains under the eyes. Lots of dogs also have **red-brown stains** on the fur of their mustaches, ears, between the toes, and at the base of the toenails. People often dismiss these stains, thinking they are just part of the way the dog is. In fact, they are not normal at all. **The reason for these brown stains? Yeast! Yuck!**

I was prompted to write this article because someone showed me the above photo of a very happy dog (Figure 1).

At first, I thought that the dog was just dirty – maybe it had been having a ball playing in the mud, much to the dismay of its person. But when I looked closer, I noticed the absence of mud on its feet. Those telltale reddish-brown stains on the mouth and ears indicate the growth of a very specific species of yeast, *Malassezia spp*. **This yeast just LOVES dogs!**

Good Yeast, Bad Yeast

Now I'm not talking about the yeast that was in such demand during COVID-19 lockdowns, as people suddenly found the time to bake their favorite bread recipes. That's good yeast. *Malassezia* is a bad yeast, at least when there is too much of it. True, it's part of the normal flora – the organisms that normally inhabit the skin. Normally the body's immune system keeps its growth in check. But when it grows out of control, it creates an imbalance in the body's homeostasis – the healthy balance of your dog's biological systems. The good news is that *Malassezia* overgrowth can be corrected.

Note the reddish-brown yeast stains on this cutie's mouth and feet.

People often dismiss these stains, thinking they are just part of the way the dog is. In fact, they are not normal at all.

Malassezia Overgrowth

There are two kinds of *Malassezia* overgrowth. Occasionally dogs will experience a massive overgrowth, in which large numbers of yeast grow on the skin and penetrate into the skin layers, causing hair loss, a darkening/reddening of the skin color and the accumulation of greasy scabs. This type of infection can be seen in dogs that have endocrine disorders, immune suppression, or allergies, all of which can alter the skin's normal barrier function. It also can occur after long-term treatment with antibiotics or steroids, causing an imbalance of the normal bacteria that live on the skin and keep it healthy. That form of *Malassezia* overgrowth demands immediate veterinary attention, and often requires treatment with topical and/or systemic anti-fungal agents.

But let's talk about the less extensive kind of *Malassezia* overgrowth that can cause milder, localized skin inflammation, ear and nail bed infections, and those unsightly stains around the eyes and on the mouth, ears, and feet. Besides the fact that those red-brown stains affect your dog's appearance, it is important to reduce the amount of *Malassezia* growing on your dog because the fungus itself is quite immunogenic. It causes your dog's body to mount an inflammatory response, which can induce a state of chronic inflammation on your dog's skin. Chronic inflammation of any organ is undesirable, and the skin is actually the largest organ in the body. Reducing the number of *Malassezia* organisms growing on your dog's skin and coat is key.

A Few of Yeast's Favorite Things

What kind of environment favors the growth of *Malassezia*? This yeast would do very well on a tropical island, because it loves moisture and warmth. Your dog's ears, facial folds (especially common in brachycephalic dogs), folds around the lips, skin between the toes, and other areas with skin folds, such as the vulva, are home, sweet home for *Malassezia*. As a result, the most important factor in reducing yeast growth is to keep these areas clean and dry. This can be done by wiping moist areas daily with an antimicrobial soap such as those containing chlorhexidine, followed by thorough drying. If your dog is a water baby, towel off their face, ears, and other susceptible locations when the water play is done.

To reduce the amount of yeast in your dog's environment, make sure you put your dog's food and water bowls in the dishwasher daily, using the sanitize setting. This will get rid of the biofilm that often covers these items and almost certainly contains yeast.

Dogs that suffer frequent yeast ear infections should be seen by a veterinarian to check for allergies or other underlying causes. In addition, I have found that shaking some Desenex® foot powder in the ears once a week can help prevent this frustrating and painful condition. The foot powder has drying and antifungal properties, which help reduce yeast growth.

No yeast on this gal!

Of course, there are some areas that are tough to keep clean and dry. This is true for dogs that produce a lot of tears. Many small dogs have plugged or very small tear ducts, which can make them tear excessively. Brachycephalic dogs frequently have large eyes and small eyelids, which cause their tears to overflow. A visit to a veterinary ophthalmologist is always warranted, to be sure that there isn't a physical reason for excessive tearing that could be corrected. Unfortunately, those chronically moist areas under the eyes can provide a perfect environmental niche for yeast growth.

What Should You Do?

While there are no peer-reviewed data on the effect of diet on tear staining, my clinical experience suggests that non-allergic dogs that have tear staining can benefit from a change from a kibble-based diet to one using fresh foods. Figure 2 shows Chloe, whose eyes were always tear-stained, even though her person cleaned them religiously every night. At that time, Chloe was fed kibble (left). The photo on the right was taken one month after Chloe was switched to a fresh, frozen dog food. Nothing else was changed. Pretty amazing!

Figure 2. Yeast stains on a dog fed kibble (left) and after one month of fresh food (right).

Warning! Avoid products that claim to clear up tear stains using an additive to your dog's food or water. Many of these contain antibiotics, which are ineffective against yeast, and can significantly upset your dog's natural gut microflora.

As you can see, with a little bit of management, you might be able to significantly reduce or even abolish those awful brown stains and even better, the yeast that cause them.

For references, see Notes, p. 142.

27. The 'Cure' in Curcumin

Soft tissue (muscle, tendon, ligament) injuries are common in active dogs. In one study of agility dogs, 87% of all injuries involved soft tissues. Muscles heal quickly and generally return to full function, but tendons and ligaments are notoriously difficult to heal and frequently resolve by deposition of scar tissue, which impairs function.

Another painful condition is osteoarthritis, thought to affect one in five adult dogs in North America, and likely an even higher proportion of active and older dogs.

Anything that claims to improve the lives of dogs with soft tissue injuries or arthritis is definitely worth checking out, so **two studies of the effects of the spice curcumin on tendon healing and arthritis caught my attention**. Earlier studies had suggested that curcumin might be used to treat chronic inflammatory illnesses such as neurodegenerative, cardiovascular, neoplastic, pulmonary, metabolic, and autoimmune diseases. So, let's check out the results of those two studies.

Effects of Curcumin on Tendon Healing
In one study, investigators examined the effects of curcumin on the healing of tendons in rats. They found that, in comparison to placebo-treated rat tendons, **curcumin-treated rat tendons had**:
1. **More organized, parallel tendon collagen fibers** as compared to the placebo-treated rat tendons' randomly oriented fibers, which resembled scar tissue (Figure 1)
2. **More type I collagen**, the main protein that gives tendons their strength
3. **Lower levels of MDA, a marker of tissue damage**
4. **Higher levels of MnSOD, a key antioxidant** that prevents tissue damage
5. **Higher tensile strength**

Ok, so it looks like curcumin can improve the speed and quality of tendon healing in rats. But what about dogs? The basic structure and function of tendons is similar in both rats and dogs, so my bet is that curcumin works the same in both species. The second study looked at the effects of curcumin in dogs.

Effects of Curcumin on Osteoarthritis in Dogs
Before we look at this study, let's take a brief trip back to basic high school biology. Remember how you learned that genes are responsible for initiating production of all the molecules in the body? Well, for these molecules to be made, genes must be first activated or "expressed." So, one way to study the body's reaction to a therapeutic is to measure the expression of various genes, and that's what was done in the second study.

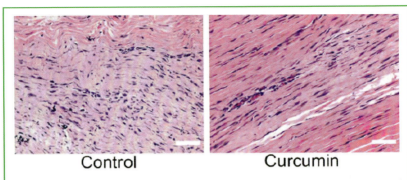

Figure 1. Curcumin-treated rat tendons (right) had more organized fibers and more protein content (indicated by the deeper pink color) than the tendons of placebo-treated rats (left).

That study compared genes that were up- or down-regulated in the white blood cells (WBC) of dogs with osteoarthritis treated either with curcumin or a nonsteroidal anti-inflammatory drug. WBCs are important because they play an active role in inflammation and healing throughout the body.

Twelve arthritic dogs were randomly assigned to two groups. Six dogs were treated with Previcox®, a nonsteroidal anti-inflammatory drug (NSAID) commonly used to reduce the pain and inflammation of arthritis. The other six were treated with curcumin at a dose of 4 mg/kg twice a day. WBCs from both groups of dogs before and 20 days after treatment were examined for the level of expression of genes that are associated with inflammation.

The results showed that curcumin essentially mimicked the anti-inflammatory and immune response activity of Previcox®. Remarkably, almost every gene that was up or down regulated by Previcox® was similarly up or down regulated by curcumin.

These studies suggest that when one of our dogs is diagnosed with a soft tissue injury such as a sprain or strain, or with arthritis, we might consider curcumin as an adjunctive therapy. One way to administer curcumin to a dog is by making Golden Paste, which is then added to the dog's meal.

Discovering the Dog
The Cure in Curcumin

Golden Paste Recipe

Ingredients
- 1 cup purified water
- 1/2 cup organic turmeric powder (plus additional to adjust consistency)
- 1/4 cup extra virgin coconut oil or other fat such as ghee or extra virgin olive oil
- 1 tsp finely ground black pepper

Method
1. Heat powdered turmeric and water on low to medium-low heat until it begins to form a thick paste.
2. Add ground pepper and fat(s) of choice and combine well, adjusting the water or turmeric quantities as needed.
3. You may also choose to add approximately 1 to 2 tablespoons of raw honey and 1 to 2 teaspoons of warming spices that pair well with turmeric such as nutmeg, curry powder, cinnamon, cardamom, or salt.
4. Once your paste is the consistency you desire, store in a glass jar with a tight-fitting lid in the refrigerator for 1 to 2 months.

There are about 200 mg of curcumin in one teaspoon of turmeric, so this recipe makes about 2,400 mg of curcumin – more if you added more turmeric to adjust the consistency. Calculate how much to give your dog based on a dose of 4 mg/kg body weight twice a day.

If you are making Golden Paste for yourself, it is recommended that you consume about 1 to 2 teaspoons of paste a day in warm water, juices, smoothies, teas, golden milks, nut butters and snacks, stir-fries, stews, dressings, and other savory foods.

For references, see Notes, p. 142.

Behavior & Training

28. To Harness or Not to Harness?
That is the Question

You might have noticed a recent uptick in the use of **harnesses as an alternative to collars**. At the same time, there has been a **concern that harnesses might affect dogs' gait or even potentially increase the risk of injuries**. Researchers in the UK investigated exactly that question by comparing the effect of restrictive and non-restrictive harnesses on the shoulder extension of dogs when walking and trotting.

There are two main **categories of harnesses**: those that are thought to be **non-restrictive** to front limb movement, which have a Y-shaped chest strap (Figure 1), and those considered **restrictive**, which have a strap that traverses the front limb (Figure 2).

Figure 1. Example of a non-restrictive harness. These have a Y-shaped component (arrow) that should lie over the manubrium (front of the sternum).

Figure 2. Example of a restrictive harness. Note the horizontal strap that traverses the front limb.

In this study, nine dogs were moved at a walk and a trot on a treadmill wearing either just a collar, a non-restrictive harness (an X-back mushing harness; Trixie Fusion harness), or a restrictive harness (Easy Walk harness). The researchers placed markers on the sides of the dogs' legs and used video cameras to **measure the angle of the shoulder when the front limb was in maximal extension** (when the foot was placed furthest forward).

Some of their **results were unexpected!**

1. Collar vs Non-Restrictive Harness vs Restrictive Harness

- Dogs wearing **only a collar had significantly more shoulder extension**, both while walking and trotting, than dogs wearing either type of harness.
- Dogs wearing **non-restrictive harnesses had significantly less shoulder extension than dogs wearing restrictive harnesses** when both walking and trotting. That was the **unexpected finding**, and we'll look more closely at that result below.

2. Weights vs No Weights
Weights were added to the harness to try to simulate the dog pulling against a harness attached to a leash held by a person. The weights were used in a way that caused the harness to be pulled up and away from the dog's back at a 45-degree angle, similar to how the harness would be pulled if a person were walking behind the dog.

- Dogs **walking** using non-restrictive harnesses with weights had significantly less shoulder extension than dogs wearing non-restrictive harnesses without weights or than those wearing restrictive harnesses with or without weights.
- Dogs **trotting** using non-restrictive harnesses with weights had significantly less shoulder extension than dogs wearing restrictive harnesses with or without weights.

The authors are to be commended for performing this important study and for their excellent discussion of the results. One limitation of the study mentioned by the authors was that their system was not designed to measure step or stride length or stance time, which can affect shoulder extension. However, a previous harness study did look at those parameters. That study showed that **both non-restrictive and restrictive harnesses alter step and stride length as compared to the same dogs wearing just a collar.**

Discovering the Dog
To Harness or Not to Harness?

Questions, Questions...

1. Why would the so-called non-restrictive harness reduce shoulder extension more than the restrictive harness?

In my opinion, it was likely a function of **harness fit**. As you can see in Figure 3 (taken from the publication but with arrows added), the non-restrictive harness is not ideally fitted to the dog. The neck straps that lie in front of the scapula (shoulder blade) are **pressing backward against the scapula, impeding its forward movement.** This, of course, would limit shoulder extension.

Non-restrictive harnesses need to be fitted so that they are tight around the dog's neck. That way, when the dog is pulling, the Y-shaped chest strap applies pressure to the stable manubrium (the front of the sternum). The straps on the side of the neck should not slide back to lie against the shoulder blade. For most dogs, the **neck part of the harness needs to be adjustable and needs to have a clip.** If it is large enough to slip over the dog's head, it probably will be too loose at the neck.

2. Why would the addition of weights to the non-restrictive harness further reduce the dog's shoulder extension?

See answer to question 1. I think that when the weights pulled on the harness, those **loose side straps** pulled even harder against the dog's shoulder blades, further restricting shoulder extension.

3. Why would the addition of weights to the restrictive harness allow the dog to have more shoulder extension?

Likely that the weights on the restrictive harness, which were set to pull at 45 degrees to horizontal, **allowed the horizontal band to rise up** on the dog's front, taking some of the pressure of that band off the shoulder joint (Figure 4). This would allow the dog to extend its shoulder further (although it might put pressure on the neck).

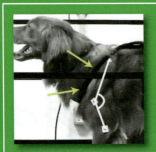

Figure 3. This shows the experimental set-up for dogs using the non-restrictive harness in this study. The white lines show how the angle of maximum shoulder extension was measured. The yellow arrows (added by this author) show the harness pressing into the dog's body in front of the scapula, which would prevent the shoulder blade from freely sliding forward when the dog is wearing this harness, This would reduce the angle of shoulder extension. (Modified from Lafuente et al, 2018)

Figure 4. This shows the experimental set-up for dogs using the restrictive harness. The yellow arrow (added by the author) indicates the direction in which the harness might move when a weight that pulls upward and backward at a 45-degree angle is attached to the harness. This would reduce pressure on the shoulder joint but might put increased pressure on the dog's neck. (Modified from Lafuente et al, 2018)

Bottom Line:
- Because two studies now provide good evidence that **both restrictive and non-restrictive harnesses alter dogs' gaits**, a collar might be a better choice for many dogs. However, dogs wearing collars should be trained to walk politely, without pulling, on a leash, as discussed in an excellent book called *My Dog Pulls. What Do I Do?* by Turid Rugaas.
- If you choose to use a **non-restrictive harness**, make sure it is **tightly fitted** around the dog's neck so that it doesn't slide back and put pressure on the dog's shoulders.
- If you choose to use a **restrictive harness**, make sure it is **loosely fitted**, so that it can slide away from the dog's shoulder as needed. But recognize that it might put pressure on your dog's neck.

> **NOTE:**
> Harnesses are a safer option for dogs that have tracheal collapse, laryngeal paralysis, obstructive airway disease, or neurological problems involving the neck, such as wobblers disease.

Correct harness fit is critical.

This non-restrictive harness fits correctly.

For references, see Notes, p. 143.

29. Love, Actually
How a Tiny Peptide Drives Our Passion for Dogs

Oxytocin. Most of us think of it as the hormone that helps bitches whelp and produce milk. And yes, it's that, but so much more. A series of recent studies have revealed how **oxytocin has a major effect on the brains of both people and dogs to strengthen the human-canine bond** – that indescribable interspecies attachment that just might explain why you're reading this.

Oxytocin is a peptide hormone that is secreted into the blood from the pituitary, a pea-sized structure at the base of the brain, although it also can be made in many other cells of the body. Its size – just nine amino acids long – truly belies its important role in how people and dogs respond to the world around them.

> *Oxytocin has a major effect on the brains of both people and dogs to strengthen the human-canine bond.*

Oxytocin plays a critical role in human communication. When a mother gazes at her infant, attachment begins to develop. You may be familiar with imprinting, in which an orphan duckling becomes attached to a human and begins to follow them around. Human attachment is a more sophisticated version of this phenomenon and is the foundation for all interpersonal relationships.

Oxytocin plays other roles in humans as well – **it's called the "love hormone"** for a reason. Oxytocin makes you feel good when you're with someone you love by stimulating the reward center in your brain, and it also reduces stress.

Recently scientists have been studying the role of oxytocin in the human-canine bond. It was already known that interactions between humans and dogs resulted in oxytocin release into the blood stream of both species. To understand more about the mechanism of this mutual hormonal response, researchers performed experiments to ask the following questions:

1. Is gaze important for mutual oxytocin release between humans and dogs like it is for mothers and infants?

2. Does mutual oxytocin release happen between humans and hand-raised wolves or just between humans and dogs?

To answer these questions, researchers measured urine oxytocin levels in dogs or hand-raised wolves and their people before and after spending 30 minutes in a room together. During that time, the dogs' people could gaze at the dogs or wolves, talk to them, and touch them.

Results: Dogs differed in the amount of time that they would gaze at their person; they were divided into long gazers and short gazers. **Long gazers induced significantly higher mutual oxytocin levels in both their people and themselves** during the 30-minute interaction, whereas short gazers and wolves did not.

Conclusion: As in the relationship between mother and child, **humans interacting with dogs experience gaze-induced mutual oxytocin secretion** and the longer the gaze, the higher the resulting oxytocin levels in both humans and dogs (and the better both feel). This hormonal interaction is called the *oxytocin-gaze positive loop*. The diagram below illustrates that steps that are involved in this positive feedback loop:

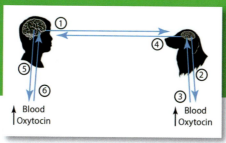

The Oxytocin-Gaze Positive Loop

Try a Little Experiment Now
Sit down and gaze into your dog's admiring eyes. Now think about how it makes you feel. It might seem silly, but just go ahead and do it. When you think about your feelings, do the words "calm," "love," "peaceful," "happy," and/or "content" come to mind? If they do, then you are experiencing the oxytocin-gaze positive loop!

As a dog lover, I am sure that you can connect with the closing statements in the researchers' publication:" These results suggest that humans may feel affection for their companion dogs similar to that felt toward human family members…" You can't help it – it's a chemical attraction!

For references, see Notes, p. 143.

30. How to Make Your Dog More Optimistic

Research across many species, in rats, zoo animals, dogs, and humans, shows that **their attitude towards life affects their welfare, mental health, ability to learn, and the quality of their decisions**. Negative attitudes in our canine companions are often tied to separation anxiety or dog-directed fear and aggression. We want our dogs to have a positive attitude not only because it makes them happier but also because it increases mental stability and improves their ability to learn and make good decisions about situations in which they find themselves. It turns out that **one dog sport improves dogs' optimism** and with it, provides all these benefits.

Cognitive bias has a significant influence on your dog's happiness.

Cognitive Bias

We all know people who are 'glass half-full' types – they look at life from a positive viewpoint and generally are fun to be with. And then there are the 'glass half-empty' types, who always seem pessimistic and can be kind of a downer to spend time with.

This attitude toward life is referred to as cognitive bias, and it has huge implications for mental health, learning, and memory. It also significantly influences behavior and decision-making. In fact, changing a person's cognitive bias is a core feature of cognitive behavioral therapy, a well-founded therapeutic intervention for improving mental health.

Cognitive bias is measured in humans using a language-based test. In contrast, cognitive bias testing in animals consists of training the animal to discriminate between two stimuli: one associated with a positive event (e.g., a food reward), the other associated with a negative event, such as disgusting food, a fear-eliciting object, or the absence of a reward. The animal is then given an ambiguous stimulus and its behavior is observed to see whether it expects the positive or negative outcome.

When tested for cognitive bias, rats living in unpredictable conditions expect more negative outcomes than rats living in predictable conditions. Sheep released from restraints develop a more positive cognitive bias. Pigs in enriched environments are more optimistic than pigs in less enriched environment. **Even honey bees demonstrate cognitive bias** – those from hives that are shaken are more likely to drink from flowers containing a liquid with less sugar as compared to bees from a stable hive.

Cognitive Bias Testing In Dogs

To test canine cognitive bias, a dog is seated about 10 ft (3 m) from a 6-ft (2-m) line placed perpendicular to the direction in which the dog and its person are facing (Figure 1). The dog is shown a bowl containing delicious treats at one end of the 6-ft line (the positive end) and an empty bowl at the other end of the 6-ft line (the negative end). An empty bowl is then placed in the middle of the 6-ft line and the dog is observed to see how many seconds it takes to approach the bowl. A dog that approaches the center-placed bowl quickly and eagerly, expecting it to contain food, has a positive cognitive bias.

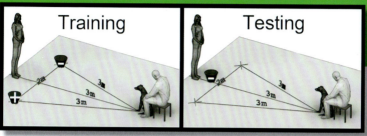

Figure 1. Cognitive bias testing in dogs. After checking out the bowl with the food (+) and without (-), the speed and eagerness with which the dog approaches the empty center-placed bowl is tested. Image modified from Duranton & Horowitz, 2019.

Cognitive Bias in Dogs Trained in Nosework vs Heeling

Cognitive bias testing was used to compare the attitude of dogs that had been trained in nosework or heeling. Twenty dogs of various breeds were trained in the cognitive bias test, so they knew where to go to get the good treats (+), and they knew that the other bowl was empty (-). The dogs were then randomly assigned to groups of 10 dogs each and all dogs were tested for their cognitive bias by placing a bowl in the ambiguous center position and recording the amount of time it took them to go and check out the bowl. There were no differences between the groups in this initial test.

One group of dogs then spent two weeks being trained in nosework, while the other group was trained in heeling. Both groups of dogs spent the same amount of time training with their people, the same amount of time being active during the day and ingested the same quantity of food during training. The groups were then re-tested for cognitive bias. The researchers measured how many seconds it took the dogs to go to the ambiguous bowl after training as compared to before training.

Extra Note

Oxytocin also improves cognitive bias in dogs. So, all that time you spend petting, making eye contact, and telling your dog you love them (which induces secretion of oxytocin in both humans and dogs) is improving both your and your dog's outlook on life. I'm all for that!

Results

Dogs that had been trained in nosework approached the ambiguous bowl significantly faster than they had previously, whereas there was no difference in speed of approach for the dogs trained in heeling. The authors concluded that the dogs that were trained in nosework had developed a more optimistic outlook. They postulated that pet dogs generally cannot engage in natural behaviors such as foraging, whereas free-range dogs spend 10% to 22% of their time investigating their environment. They quote several studies demonstrating that foraging is a natural behavior of many species including dogs and is a form of environmental enrichment important for animal welfare. **Presumably nosework recapitulates a dog's foraging experience**.

Dogs that were trained in nosework had a more optimistic outlook on life.

OK, I know what you're thinking – the dogs that were trained in nosework were clearly trained to look into containers for food, so of course they went more quickly towards the ambiguous bowl in hopes of finding food. Well, it should be noted that the dogs in both groups were just as effective in identifying, and approaching or not, the positive and negative bowls during the cognitive bias testing – only their behavior towards the ambiguous bowl differed. That suggests that there wasn't an effect of being trained to go and investigate bowls.

How cool is that? **Playing scenting games such as nosework with our dogs improves their outlook on life**. If dogs are like other species, that optimistic attitude will increase their mental stability, speed up their learning process, and improve their decision-making abilities. I bet some of that optimism is bound to rub off on us too!

Take-Home Message

Foraging (looking for and consuming food) is stimulating and intrinsically rewarding to dogs. Thus, **increasing your dog's foraging time, whether that means teaching formal nosework/scent work or just as a game to play around the house and yard, or using food-distributing toys might, in fact, increase your dog's optimism and outlook toward life**. Isn't that a great gift to give?

For references, see Notes, p. 143.

31. Scents of Success

The extraordinary olfactory abilities of dogs have long been used by humans for odor identification and discrimination. Our use of this incredible canine tool, which we are completely unable to imitate or engineer, is continuously expanding. **We deploy the canine nose for life-and-death activities** such as improving our safety (e.g., bomb and drug detection, tracking lost individuals, avalanche work) and our health (e.g., cancer detection, low blood sugar alerts). **We also use the dog's exceptional scenting ability for recreation** as we hunt live game and play novel games involving scent detection (e.g., nose/scent work, barn hunt, obedience, tracking, hunt tests/field trials, etc.).

Given the importance of the dog's superlative schnoz, it's important to understand what factors might alter its function. What about physical stressors such as exercise, conditioning, diet, and environment?

Several studies provide important information about what dogs need to be at their scenting best. They also reveal clues about how we can optimize our dogs' olfaction.

Factors That Affect Scents-Ability in Dogs
1. Conditioning
Some people are surprised that conditioning can affect a dog's scenting ability. I mean, what does the strength of a dog's muscles have to do with the ability of odor molecules to land on the receptors in the nose and transmit a neurological signal to the brain? Nonetheless, fitness is one of the most important factors in your dog's odor detection ability. In one study, **dogs that were less fit had an astounding 64% reduction in their scent sensitivity** compared to physically conditioned dogs. Another study showed **a higher frequency of correct target alerts in physically fit dogs**. This might be related in part to the lower heart rate in conditioned dogs and therefore a reduction in the need for panting (which reduces olfaction because of reduced airflow through the nose).

2. Diet
Studies of the effects of diet on scenting ability in dogs offer some fascinating insights into the potential for improving scenting ability through appropriate nutrition. English Pointers withheld from exercise and fed a diet supplemented with coconut oil

experienced compromised olfaction, but exercised dogs maintained their olfactory acuity – another reason to keep your dog fit!

Another study showed benefits to olfaction in dogs fed a corn oil-supplemented diet and exercised – there's that fitness component again! A third study looked at "the breakfast effect," in which dogs searched more accurately 30 min following the consumption of breakfast than when fasted. They concluded that food might provide energy for cognitive processes, and that search accuracy in fasted dogs decreased because of energy depletion.

3. Environment
Any source of heat stress, including lack of acclimatization to a novel environment, increased environmental temperature, increased humidity, lack of access to water, and/or poor ventilation, **contributes to reduced odor detection ability**. A dog that is heat stressed will pant, which reduces olfaction due to reduced airflow through the nose. In addition, dehydration can significantly decrease odor detection capabilities in dogs.

4. Age
Older dogs can have age-related changes in their scenting system, similar to those experienced by elderly people. Older dogs had a reduced number of odor-detecting cells in their noses and the cells that remained had a reduced number of cilia (the tiny hairs that grab odor molecules out of the air). Scent detection games can provide excellent environmental stimulation for older dogs, though, so don't let this possible deficiency stop you from providing your oldster with odoriferous experiences. Just make sure the odors are strong!

5. Drugs
There is a long list of pharmaceuticals that can cause reduced scenting ability in humans, including anesthetics, antiarrhythmics, antihistamines, antimicrobials, antiproliferative and immuno-suppressive drugs, endocrine drugs, gastrointestinal drugs, neurologic drugs, and non-steroidal anti-inflammatory drugs. The list of drugs that have been proven to affect scenting ability in dogs is shorter because of a lack of research. Those include some cardiac drugs, high doses of metronidazole, steroids, and chemotherapeutics. Regardless, it is important to consider **that any dog being treated with a pharmaceutical might have diminished scenting ability**.

6. Subclinical or Chronic Diseases

Interestingly, **endocrine conditions such as hypothyroidism, diabetes, and Cushing's disease can reduce scenting ability in dogs**. The mechanism for this is unknown but given that many dogs live with these diseases, it is important to ensure that your dog is getting the best therapy for any possible chronic condition. This should minimize the risk of effects on olfaction. **If your dog is living with one of these conditions, consider that they might be less efficient at scenting**.

Take-Home Message

It might seem worrisome that there are so many factors that can affect your dog's scents-ability, but the good news is that with a little knowledge and forethought, you can substantially reduce the risk of odor detection deficiencies and even help your dog establish and maintain the best possible scenting skills!

For references, see Notes, p. 144.

32. Cold Nose, Warm Sense
Your Dog has a Newly Discovered Superpower!

Chaoss

Did you know that your dog has something in common with vampire bats, pit vipers, and black fire beetles? What could that possibly be?

It all started when some scientists from Sweden and Hungary went into a bar....

Well, that might not be exactly true. I'm not sure where they were when they got together and asked the question, "Why is a dog's nose moist and cold, when most other mammals' noses are warm and dry?" No doubt this is a question that has also kept you awake many a night....

They knew that the dog's rhinarium, the area of nose surrounding the nostrils, has numerous glands that secrete moisture, and under the skin there is a dense network of nerve fibers that connect to the trigeminal nerve, the largest nerve in the head. Normally, receptors on the face sense touch and pain, as well as the positions of the muscles of the face (such as when your dog smiles) and transmit that information via the trigeminal nerve to the brain. So, the scientists asked, "What information might all those nerves under the skin of the nose be transmitting via that same trigeminal nerve?"

A Clue From Snakes
Being interested in all things animal, the scientists knew that pit vipers, such as rattlesnakes, have so-called pit organs on the sides of their faces that are moist and colder than the snake's skin. They help the snake sense differences in temperature, just like a thermal imaging camera.

They are so sensitive that they can detect differences of as little as 1/1000 of a degree. With the help of the pit organ, even in the dark, a snake can sense the warmth of a nearby rodent (Figure 1) so that it can strike its prey more accurately.

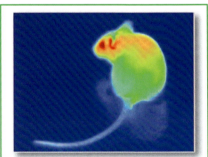
Figure 1. A viper's pit organ helps the snake sense the warmth of a nearby rodent.

Hmmmm...
Dogs' noses are wet and colder than the rest of their bodies (Figure 2). Might those noses help dogs sense temperature differences just like in snakes?

The Experiments
To test this, the scientists in Sweden trained three dogs of a variety of sizes and breeds to get a food reward if they pushed a sliding panel that was very slightly warm. The dogs did not receive a reward if they pushed a neutral temperature panel. They then tested the dogs in a double-blind study in which neither the dog nor the handler knew which panel was warm. The results showed that the dogs were consistently able to detect the warmer panel with very high accuracy.

The scientists in Hungary then took over. They took 13 dogs that were trained to lie still in an fMRI unit and presented them with either a warm or a neutral temperature box. They then checked the fMRI images to see what part of the dogs' brains were processing that information.

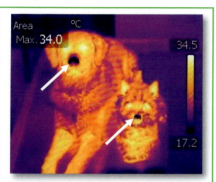

Figure 2. Thermal image of two dogs – a Golden Retriever (left) and a Norwich Terrier (right), showing their dark noses (arrows), which are several degrees colder than other parts of their bodies.

When the dogs were presented with the neutral temperature box, their brains showed no activity. However, when presented with the warm box, a discrete area on the left side of the brain lit up, indicating that the experience of sensing something warm was being processed in that area. As it happens, that area of the brain is where many different types of sensory information are processed so that the animal can plan specific, targeted movements. The most common reason for these movements is to capture prey.

These studies demonstrated for the first time that dogs really do have a 6th sense – the ability to detect heat. The only other species currently known to be able to accurately sense infrared radiation are the black fire beetle, certain snake species, and one other species of mammal so far, the vampire bat.

The Take-Home Message
How might the ability to sense heat be important to us? Most of our dogs are homebodies, preferring to get their prey in the form of tasty meals provided to them twice a day with no more effort than looking hungry or giving their people a nudge or two. Nonetheless, I can envision several situations in which this ability might be useful for our canine companions.

This heat-sensing ability might be used by bitches with pups during the first few weeks of their lives. Not only might it help them locate their puppies in low-lighting conditions, but perhaps it also helps them recognize when one of their puppies is fading or has passed away.

We also know that newborn puppies are thermotropic, moderating their body temperature by moving towards or away from sources of heat, like their mother.

However, until now we've never known how these relatively helpless and limited babies accomplish this. Perhaps this canine 6th sense is present at birth and enables puppies to find their dam's warm body and even warmer nipples, which they do very quickly after birth.

I imagine that **this sense might also be used by dogs participating in the sports of barn hunt and earthdog** in which dogs must find a living rat. Although the sense of smell will also be used, this ability to sense radiant heat might help dogs home in on their prey faster, particularly terriers searching in dark, underground earthdog tunnels. It is **likely that heat sensing is also used by hunting dogs**, particularly the pointers, setters, and spaniels, who must detect and point out live, and therefore warm, gamebirds while hunting over large tracts of land. **Search and rescue dogs may also be aided by this ability** as they locate missing or trapped humans in the wilderness or at disaster sites. We already knew the canine nose was amazing, but this research elevates our dogs' schnozzes to superhero status.

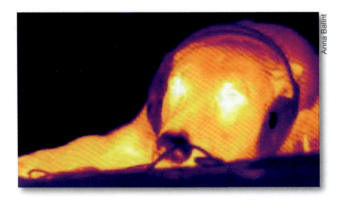

For references, see Notes, p. 145.

33. On the One Hand...
Paw Preference & Your Dog's Emotions

Does your dog prefer to hold his Kong™ toy with one paw rather than the other as he licks out the delicious contents? Does your dog push the bathroom door open with one paw in preference to the other as she plots to invade your privacy? **Most dogs, like most humans, have a paw preference** and, just like humans, more (about 2/3) are right-sided than left.

This in-built feature is called *laterality* and it has been studied in many different species, from picas to primates, and of course, in our best friends. Laterality derives from the fact that the two hemispheres of the brain have evolved to have specialized functions. The **right brain specializes in detecting novelty and the expression of intense emotions** such as aggression and fear – it activates "fight or flight" responses. In contrast, the **left brain responds to routine experiences and calming stimuli.**

An **easy way to judge whether a dog is right-pawed or left-pawed** is to note which front leg the dog advances first when moving forward down a set of steps from a position with both forelegs level (Figure 1).

Figure 1. (A) Start position. Dog showing (B) right paw preference and (C) left paw preference. Test is performed with the handler on both sides of the dog. (From Tomkins *et al*, 2010)

Sensory Lateralization
Interestingly, dogs have laterality not only in their paw use, but when using other senses including vision, hearing, and olfaction (scent).

Vision. When an **alarming stimulus** (a cat in a defensive posture) was shown to dogs, they contracted the left neck muscles, thus **turning their heads to the left**, indicating that the right brain was responding to the arousing stimulus. **Note**: the two halves of the brain drive motor functions on the opposite sides of the body.

> *Dogs with a strong paw preference were more confident.*

Hearing. When dogs were presented with **audio recordings of a thunderstorm**, dogs preferentially **turned their heads to the left** suggesting an alarm-based response. In contrast, they turned their heads to the right when hearing the familiar sound of dog vocalizations.

Olfaction. Dogs **used the right nostril** (which is controlled by the right brain) **when sniffing an arousing odor** such as adrenaline. When a non-aversive odor such as food was used, dogs sniffed with the right nostril initially because the odor was novel. However, scenting shifted to the left nostril on subsequent presentations of the odor.

Paw Preference and Emotions

Dogs' paw preferences can have different strengths. Some dogs use the same paw much more consistently for a given task, while others have a weaker preference, sometimes using one paw, and sometimes the other. One study showed that **dogs with weaker paw preference showed more stress behaviors** when exposed to threatening noises. In contrast, **dogs with stronger paw preferences were more confident** and relaxed in unfamiliar environments and when presented with novel stimuli.

Interestingly, it appears that the amplitude of tail wagging (the distance over which the tail wags) is related to the level of emotional arousal the dog is experiencing. Dogs wagged their tails to the right when presented with both their person and a neutral stranger, but the **wagging response to the dog's person had greater amplitude**.

In another series of studies, scientists examined how dogs wagged their tails in response to different situations designed to evoke different emotions. When dogs were presented with an unfamiliar dog showing clear antagonistic behavior, the dogs wagged their tails more to the left. **When presented with a positive emotional stimulus, such as their person, the dogs again wagged their tails more to the right**.

Take-Home Message

Laterality in dogs might provide us with **new insights into their emotional lives and might even help us predict a dog's behavior or help dogs adapt to stressful situations**. For example, right-pawed dogs were found to be more successful in completing guide dog training than left-pawed or ambidextrous dogs (4). Perhaps strength of paw preference might be used to assess vulnerability to stress of dogs in shelters. Studies of lateralization continue to reveal new insights into our understanding of canine cognition, and that can only help improve our relationships with this species that does so much for us.

For references, see Notes, p. 145.

34. The Eyes Have It
Specifically, Dog Eyes Do, and Wolf Eyes Don't

Let me explain. Scientists in the UK and US examined in detail the facial muscles, especially the muscles around the eyes, of dogs and wolves.

It turns out that **there are two prominent muscles that move the dog's eyelids that many wolves don't have**, or if they do, they are vestigial – smaller and weaker. The first one, called the *levator anguli occuli medialis* or LAOM for short (why do we *still* use Latin names for muscles?) lifts the medial (nearest the nose) part of the dog's eyebrow up. Epic is using those muscles in the image to the left.

The second muscle, called the *retractor anguli occuli lateralis* or RAOL, pulls the outside corner of the dog's eyelid towards the ear, making the eye look larger and exposing some of the *sclera* – the white part of the eye.

Those two muscles are shown in red in Figure 1, with the dog's facial muscles illustrated on the left and the wolf's on the right. Notice how, when the LAOM contracts, it makes the inner part of the eyebrow lift and when the RAOL contracts, it makes the opening of the eyelid wider.

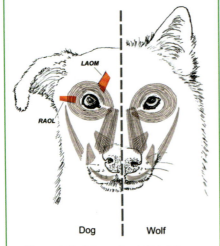

Figure 1. Facial muscles in the dog (left) and wolf (right) illustrating the two additional ocular muscles in the dog.
LAOM = *levator anguli occuli medialis*
RAOL = *retractor anguli occuli lateralis*
(From Kaminski *et al*, 2019)

Those two tiny muscles might have played a critical role in the evolution of the wolf into human's best friend.

Your Dog Is Watching

Dogs are remarkable in their ability to read our body language, including our facial features and expressions, to communicate with us. **Dogs, but not wolves, establish eye contact with humans when they cannot solve a problem**. And the gaze between humans and dogs results in mutual release of oxytocin, known as the "love hormone" (see Chapter 29).

Human-eyes-ing

Humans use eyebrow movements when they want to emphasize certain words or phrases. Remember how your friends' eyebrows moved closer together as they tried to solve a math problem in school? That's how we got the term "knitted eyebrows." And surely you recall your parents' eyebrows lifting when, as a teenager, you were caught coming home much later than you had promised!

When people are looking for important points in others' speech, they tend to focus on the upper facial area, and particularly the eyes. Interestingly, people pay attention to the same area when looking at pictures of dogs. One study showed that when humans lift their inner eyebrows, it makes them seem sad. Further studies have shown that **humans are attracted to large eyes**, like human babies have, and that we prefer interacting with animals that have visible sclera (the whites of the eye).

The Caregiver Response

Here's how these canine anatomical features and our focus on the eyes for communication might have played a role in how a fearsome predator (the wolf) evolved into that warm, furry creature that sleeps on your bed at night.

Imagine you are a member of a hunter-gatherer tribe 33,000 years ago. A wolf walks by and looks at you with curiosity. Since it is one of the wolves that has vestigial LAOM and RAOL muscles, it raises its eyebrows and widens its eyes just a bit. You (consciously or not) think that it looks just a tiny bit like a human baby (large-appearing eyes), or at least that it looks sad (elevated inner eyebrows). You have a caregiver response (your body releases oxytocin), and you leave some food out for the wolf. The wolf stays nearby, breeds with another wolf with similar facial features that is also getting handouts, and they have offspring that have larger and stronger LAOM and RAOL muscles. Just a few millennia later, you have the dog.

To strengthen the credibility of this scenario, a recent study showed that **dogs with this sad-eyed appearance were more likely to be rehomed from shelters**. Humans clearly are suckers for puppy-dog eyes!

One thing that the study didn't mention, but that must have come to your mind already, is this: Could this be the reason that so many breeds have cute little dots of a contrasting color on their medial eyebrows? Think about all the breeds of dogs with black and tan or tricolor markings like my pal, Epic, pictured at the beginning of this chapter. Did we also select for this coloration to emphasize those eyebrow communications? I'm betting we did! **Yes, the eyes definitely have it!**

For references, see Notes, p. 146.

35. Be-Yawn Compare
Is Yawning in Dogs a Sign of Empathy or Distress?

Picture this: you're riding in a car with a friend, and she yawns. A few seconds later, you yawn too, even though you're not tired or bored. Your friend yawns again and this time you decide you are going to resist yawning. But you can feel the darn yawn building in your throat until you just have to let it out! In fact, you might be stifling a yawn just from reading this! Congratulations – you're human.

Contagious yawning affects about 45% to 60% of healthy adult humans. It is thought to be associated with our capacity for empathy, so pat yourself on the back if you just yawned…

When people yawn contagiously, neural networks responsible for empathy and social skills are activated. In addition, **people who score higher on self-recognition, theory of mind, and empathy are more susceptible to yawn contagiously**. Further, the contagious effect of yawning is impaired in subjects suffering from empathy disorders, such as autism. Well, it turns out that dogs also yawn contagiously.

Contagious Yawning in Dogs
The first study to show contagious yawning in dogs demonstrated that a whopping **72% of the dogs yawned after observing a human experimenter yawn**. Interestingly, in both humans and dogs, just the sound of a yawn can elicit a yawning response. But yawning in dogs can also indicate mild to moderate stress, and until now, none of the studies showing contagious yawning in dogs had ruled this out as a possible reason for the dogs' yawning.

The authors of this study therefore set two goals:

1. To replicate contagious yawning in dogs
2. To determine whether the yawning was related to empathy or was a stress-related response

Twenty-five adult dogs of a variety of breeds and mixed breeds were used in this study, with equal numbers of males and females. Dogs were exposed to their person or an unfamiliar human either yawning or making a control open-mouth movement. At the same time, the dogs' heart rates were measured by telemetry (remote measurement) to evaluate stress.

The study **confirmed that dogs do yawn contagiously in response to humans and that, as in humans, it is most likely an empathetic response**. Dogs yawned in response to the true yawn significantly more often than to the control mouth movement, and they yawned significantly more often in response to their person yawning than to an unfamiliar person (Figure 1). Apparently, at least in this study, **contagious yawning was not related to stress** as the dogs' heart rates did not vary during any of the conditions.

Evidence of a Deep Bond

Many species experience contagious yawning with others of their own species. For example, many different species of primates other than humans (chimpanzees, bonobos, gelada baboons, and stump-tailed macaques) demonstrate contagious yawning. Budgies, a small parrot, also experience contagious yawning with other budgies. (I never even realized budgies could yawn!)

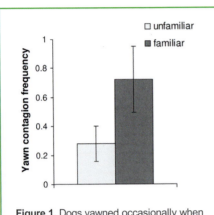

Figure 1. Dogs yawned occasionally when an unfamiliar person yawned, but significantly more often when their person yawned.

> *Dogs do not experience contagious yawning with each other, only when exposed to a yawning human.*

Interestingly, **dogs do not experience contagious yawning with each other, only when exposed to a yawning human**. The authors suggest that contagious yawning of dogs in response to humans might have evolved as an adaptation for communicating with us. This study is a contribution to the scientific basis for the therapeutic effect of dogs and as further evidence of the ability of these incredible creatures with which we share our lives to deeply empathize with us. How lucky we are!

For references, see Notes, p. 146.

36. Teacher's Pet
How to Make Sure Your Training Doesn't Go in One Ear and Out the Other

Have you ever parked outside a restaurant or concert, had an exciting few hours, and then walked outside to realize you have no idea where you left your car? Why can we easily recall our childhood telephone number but forget something we knew just a short time earlier?

Just like us, dogs have short-term and long-term memory. Short-term memory helps us remember where we parked, or where to go next on an agility course. It helps your dog remember where he put the bully stick he was enjoying before he had to leap up and bark at the door when the doorbell rang.

When we train our dogs, we want what they learn to persist much longer than a few hours. To accomplish this, those lessons need to be placed in long-term memory. Numerous studies have shown that reward-based training is the most effective way for dogs to learn. Dogs trained with positive reinforcement and without aversives are less stressed, which permits optimal learning. If you have ever tried to memorize some facts with your boss or teacher staring at you, you know that's true.

A recent study examined what kinds of post-training activities will help your dog send those newly learned lessons into long-term storage.

The Study Design
Researchers in Hungary undertook a relatively simple, but fascinating, study. Figure 1 outlines the study design. They took 53 dogs of a variety of breeds and mixed breeds that knew how to "sit" and "down" in response to cues spoken in Hungarian. They then

had their people train the sit and down using cues in English. The dogs were tested to be sure they had learned the new cues and were then divided into four groups of 12 to 14 dogs each.

One group spent the hour after training sleeping in the person's car in the parking lot. A second group was taken for a 1-hour relaxed on-leash walk through a college campus. Dogs in a third group were taught additional new English commands in 10-min sessions, and dogs in a fourth group played with a Kong™ toy while lying on the floor. The dogs were retested for their ability to correctly respond to the English sit and down cues immediately (short-term memory) and one week later (long-term memory).

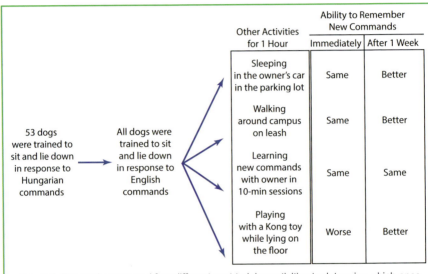

Figure 1. The study compared four different post-training activities to determine which ones improved or impaired learning retention.

The Results

Dogs that spent the hour after learning sleeping, walking, or learning new commands, all retained their ability to respond to the English sit and down commands in the short term. The dogs that played with the Kong™ toy were not as effective in responding to the new cues. The experimenters' interpretation was that because the playing had caused more arousal, dogs were less focused during the retesting session.

A week later, the dogs were retested on their responses to the English cues. Interestingly, **dogs that that slept, walked, or played after learning had significantly better performance on the long-term memory test**. In contrast, the performance of the dogs that spent time with additional training after the initial training period did not have good long-term retention.

Take-Home Message

The results of this study suggest that when dogs experience a different activity after a training session, whether that involves physical activity or sleep, their retention improves in the long term. They also suggest that an overly long or complex teaching session may interfere with consolidation of learned materials into long-term memory.

This study confirms what the best trainers have long observed and known intuitively; that **training sessions should be kept relatively short and focused – no more than 20 minutes to work on one or two concepts.**

The study also confirms that **consolidation of new knowledge will occur under a variety of circumstances and that dogs don't necessarily have to be crated or rested after a training session**, as some have proposed.

So go train your dog for a few minutes and then take a saunter, play a game of fetch, or spend some couch time together watching television. You can even drive to your favorite park and go for a Good for the Soul hike together. Just don't forget where you parked your car!

For references, see Notes, p. 147.

37. Perfect Practice Doesn't Make Perfect
Imperfect Practice Does

Remember the first time you had to give a presentation in public? You probably wrote down what you wanted to say, then practiced by reading it out loud over and over, repeating the words just as you wanted to say them in the presentation. It was very boring, and you were thinking, "How often do I need to do this before it will stick in my head?"

Researchers at Johns Hopkins' Department of Rehabilitation Medicine studying how people learn made an interesting discovery. They found out that the adage, "perfect practice makes perfect," was not quite true. Whether it's memorizing a presentation or learning how to do a front cross in agility, it turns out that we learn faster if we don't practice perfectly. Let me explain….

How Dogs Learn
When we are first learning something new, neuronal pathways send messages to an area of the brain where they are stored. **The more pathways that deliver information to the memory storage area, the more permanent those memories become**.

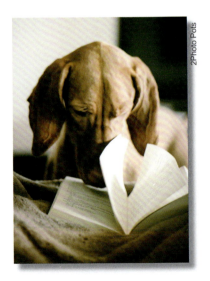

Here's an analogy. There is a huge parking lot on the south end of Baltimore with an elevated highway nearby. When you drive by that parking lot, you can see hundreds, if not thousands, of cars, all identical except for their different colors. These cars arrive by train and are offloaded and then parked in incredibly neat rows – row after row of the same make and model of car. As the train keeps delivering cars, the lot gradually gets full (Figure 1).

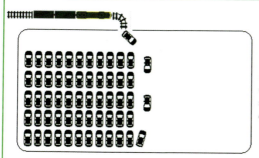

Figure 1. The train that delivers the cars is like a neuronal pathway sending information to your brain, one car at a time

The train that delivers the cars is like a neuronal pathway sending information to your brain. If that pathway keeps providing information, the brain area for storing that information will eventually become full. That's why, if you practice a presentation many times, you eventually memorize it.

Learning Faster

But the Hopkins researchers found that if you also practice slightly modified versions of a task, you learn faster than if you keep practicing the exact same thing multiple times in a row. The scientific term for this process is *memory reconsolidation*. So, let's return to the example of that presentation that you want to perfect. If you sometimes read it as fast as you can, and other times you read it slowly, leaving pauses for emphasis at various points, and other times you practice with a different projector or holding a microphone, you would, in fact, memorize the presentation faster.

Using our analogy again, picture multiple train tracks leading to the car parking lot. Perhaps there is also a ship in the harbor nearby and it is bringing cars from foreign manufacturers. All the cars are arriving at the lot, but they are entering via slightly different locations. That would allow the lot to fill up much faster (Figure 2).

Interestingly, **the process of memory reconsolidation takes about six hours**. As a result, the slight changes in the way the task is presented can't be made all at the same time – they must occur with gaps of at least six hours. As a result, **perfect learning takes time**. This process of memory reconsolidation works for both informational learning (learning facts and concepts) and for motor learning (perfecting movements).

Training Tip

How might this research apply to training our canine companions? Let's look at a dog learning 2-on, 2-off (2o2o) contacts in agility. This is a technique in which the dog stops with their two front feet on the ground and two back feet on a contact obstacle such as an A-frame, dogwalk, or teeter. Typically, we would initially use a travel board (a 3-ft long by 10-inch-wide board that is elevated about four inches off the ground). We would lure the dog onto the board and when the dog steps off so that its two front feet are on the ground, but its back feet remain on the board, we'd praise and give a treat. If we always stood beside the board when we trained, the dog would learn 2o2o contacts given enough repetition.

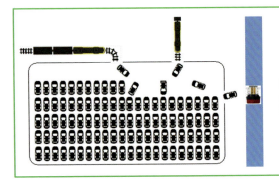

Figure 2. With multiple sources of delivery (two trains and one boat), the parking lot fills up faster.

But if, as we train over several days, we shift our position to one or the other side of the board, and we also run past the board, or send the dog to the board ahead of us, the dog will learn how to do 2o2o contacts faster. In training, we often wait to make these types of changes until late in the learning stage, once we feel that the dog knows the task well. We call that "proofing." But the Hopkins research suggests that if you introduce slight variations early in the process, learning occurs substantially faster.

But note, the changes you make in the training picture must be slight – they cannot be massive deviations in the task, or the learning speed declines, as if, using our analogy, the train tracks veered away from the parking lot.

You also can use this principle for anything you'd personally like to learn quickly, whether it's an agility move, perfect footwork in rally or obedience, or the words to your favorite song. Isn't this great news? You don't have to be perfect! In fact, it's better to be a little imperfect!

A dog doing a 2o2o contact on the agility dogwalk

For references, see Notes, p. 147.

38. Is Your Dog a Social Butterfly?

What makes a dog a dog – that gregarious canine companion? People have been asking that for a very long time. Why is it that when you raise wolves with human care and companionship from the time they are born, while they are more comfortable around humans than wolves not raised with people, they never truly become man's/woman's best friend?

How did dogs morph into becoming members of our extended families and part of our workforce? The answer to this question would help us better understand the nature of the human-canine bond and might hold the key to the process of domestication itself.

For decades, researchers believed that wolves with better social skills were gradually selected to live with humans and eventually evolved into dogs. In that model, the difference between dogs and wolves is that dogs have greater behavioral plasticity – they are better able to modify their behavior than wolves. However, recent data suggest that wolves raised by humans can behave in a similar manner to dogs in social situations, indicating that they may be more socially flexible than previously believed.

Social Behavior
A group of scientists at Princeton University and the National Institutes of Health decided to take **a genetic approach to understanding the domestication of dogs**. They compared the genomes of groups of animals with widely different characteristics – in this case, social behavior.

They first surveyed the entire genomes of 701 dogs from 85 breeds and 92 grey wolves. This analysis revealed an area on chromosome 6 that was quite different between dogs and wolves. Interestingly, mutations of the genes in this region in humans is associated with a congenital disease called Williams-Beuren Syndrome (WBS) that is characterized by hyper-sociability. Affected people have an outgoing personality and interact readily with strangers without filter or restraint, like many dogs (think wet Golden Retrievers). The researchers recognized that **a major difference between dogs and wolves is the exaggerated gregariousness of dogs and their increased propensity to initiate social contact**, even with a different species. Perhaps they were on to something!

Now the researchers needed to see whether those genetic differences between dogs and wolves on chromosome 6 corresponded with differences in social behavior. They used a well-validated test of social behavior to compare domestic dogs (of several breeds) and captive, human-socialized wolves. The dogs or wolves were given two minutes to open a puzzle box containing summer sausage (yum!) in a room with a neutral stranger present. They recorded the amount of time that was spent looking to the human for help solving the puzzle. Not surprisingly, **dogs spent significantly more time than wolves looking to the human for assistance**, a trait that they referred to as hyper-sociability.

Dog Breeds Differ

Interestingly (but not surprisingly), the study also showed that **different dog breeds vary in the amount to which they look to humans**. Some breeds were more likely to ask a human for help, while others worked more independently (see table below). Yes, there's a dog for everyone!

> *Dogs spent significantly more time than wolves looking to humans for help.*

Breeds That Looked for Help	Breeds That Worked More Independently
Bernese Mountain Dog	Basenji
Border Collie	Cairn Terrier
Boxer	Great Pyrenees
Golden Retriever	Malamute
Jack Russell Terrier	Miniature Schnauzer
Miniature Poodle	New Guinea Singing Dog
Pug	Pariah Dog
	Saluki
	Village Dogs from Puerto Rico

Wolves Raised by Humans

In contrast, wolves, even those raised by people, were much less likely to look to the human for assistance that were the dogs, thus taking the "nurture" component out of the equation.

What About Chromosome 6?

Now that the researchers had their behavioral test, they examined whether this behavioral characteristic correlated with genetic changes in the area of the canine genome on chromosome 6 that correlated with hyper-sociability in humans. And the long and short of it is, they did correlate.

It turns out that **the more hyper-social the dog was, the more their genes in that area of chromosome 6 were disrupted, or inactive**. The disruptions appeared to be caused by jumping genes (also known as transposable elements), sneaky little pieces of the DNA that jump from one area of the chromosome to another.

When that happens, the genes that are interrupted are unable to produce the protein they were designed to. **The more of these jumping genes that were inserted in that area of chromosome 6, the greater percentage of time the dogs looked to humans for help solving the puzzle**.

We don't yet know the exact functions of the genes in that area of chromosome 6, or how they might relate to sociability in dogs. But there are hints. **One of the genes produces a protein that controls the release of oxytocin when humans are in a social situation**. We know that oxytocin is released in both dogs and humans when they interact, so this might be one way in which the genes in this area might modulate the human-animal bond.

As I was writing this article, I was competing at a Nosework trial with my inexperienced Norwich Terrier, Helix. On the outdoor search, he ran up to a stack of chairs, bounced his front feet up onto the stack, sniffed it and looked at me expectantly. I called, "Alert," – a signal from the handler to the judge that the hide was found. But guess what? There was no hide there. He was just demonstrating hyper-sociability by looking to me for help. What a timely example! So, I just made a mental note to study his body language better, felt the oxytocin flowing through my body (because working together as a team is so much fun, and besides, he got all the other hides that day), and moved on. After all, he can't help it! It's genetic!

For references, see Notes, p. 147.

39. Who is That Dog In the Mirror?

Does Your Dog Think About Itself?
How we perceive ourselves, or our self-image, greatly influences how we think, feel, and relate to the rest of the world. You recognize, for example, that you have a physical body, and you might describe yourself as tall, short, athletic, or clumsy. You also know that you have a social self – one that interacts with different individuals and groups in different ways, depending on the situation.

The concept of "self" was frequently thought to be limited to humans and just a few other species, but not dogs. No longer!

Recent studies have demonstrated what those of us who share our lives with these incredible creatures have known innately all along – **dogs also have a sense of self.** Here's how the studies were done, and what it means to your relationship with your canine companions.

The Mirror Mark Test
This test, first published in the '70s, was thought by many to be the definitive test for determining whether an animal had the most basic of self-concepts – the ability to recognize that it has a body. The test is quite simple – place an animal in front of a mirror and watch how it behaves. Once the animal is used to the mirror, put a mark on part of its body that cannot be viewed without the aid of the mirror, such as under its chin. Now observe whether the animal is curious about the mark and whether it recognizes that the mark is not part of itself by scratching at it, for example.

We've all seen what puppies do in front of mirrors. They bark at the dog, they might go up and sniff at the dog's reflection, but they don't seem to recognize the dog as themselves. In fact, the ability to recognize "self" takes time to develop – humans don't pass this test until they are about two years old.

Over time, however, some scientists have felt that this test wasn't a sufficient demonstration of the concept of "self," because it depended solely on the animal's vision. What if some animals used other senses, such as scent or touch to recognize "self?" For example, in one study dogs investigated their own odors longer than those of other dogs in a type of "olfactory mirror" test. So, researchers designed a different test for dogs' recognition of self.

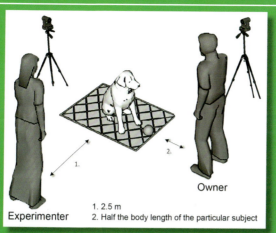

Figure 1. Dogs were asked to pick up a ball that was attached to a mat on which they were sitting. Dogs consistently realized that they had to get off the mat to pick up the ball, indicating that they had a concept of their physical bodies. (Modified from Lenkei *et al*, 2021)

The 'Body As An Obstacle' Test

In this test, toddlers that are sitting on a blanket are asked to pick up the blanket and give it to someone. Until they are about two years of age, toddlers don't realize that they have to actually get off the blanket to hand it over, suggesting that they have no concept of themselves as a physical being.

In the present study, this test was adapted to dogs. Thirty-two dogs of different breeds and sizes were asked to pick up a ball that was attached to a mat on which they were standing and give it to their person (Figure 1). These results were compared to what happened when the ball was unattached to anything or when it was attached to the ground. **Dogs consistently realized that they had to get off the mat to be able to pick up the ball, indicating that they had a concept of their own bodies as an impediment to the task.**

What Does This Mean?

When I first read this study, my reaction was, "So what?" Maybe you feel the same way. I had to delve a lot deeper to understand what it means to have a concept of "self."

How we think about ourselves determines how we relate to the world and is intimately connected to the feelings we experience such as happiness, confidence, fear, depression, and many others. It also determines how we relate to others, and how we adapt to events that occur in our lives.

Without a concept of "self," animals are believed to be unable to understand how others feel and how to interact with them based on those feelings. This new study adds to the evidence, and frankly to what we have innately known all along, that **our canine companions do have complex cognitive abilities and emotions such as empathy, trust, the ability to understand others' emotions**, and yes, even to love.

Maybe this is why your dog puts its head on your lap and looks into your eyes when you feel discouraged. Perhaps this explains why a normally hyperactive Yorkie lies still on the bed beside a cancer patient. It might even explain why your dog trots into a room full of guests carrying your underwear! It certainly does reveal that we have only scratched the surface in our understanding of our dogs' capacity for emotions. No wonder those of us who share our lives with dogs, have long recognized these marvelous beings as bona fide family members!

For references, see Notes, p. 147.

40. Can We Talk About the Ideal Family Dog?
Co-Authored by Gayle Watkins PhD*

Courtney Coles

The swift, intense demand for dogs in North America during the COVID-19 pandemic came as a surprise to many of us who already shared our lives with canine companions. It was as if the whole continent suddenly developed a visceral need to experience the comfort of this species that has shared a relationship with humans for millennia. Shelters were emptied of adoptable dogs, and breeders were overwhelmed with requests.

As dog aficionados for decades, we watched this movement with intense interest. How will it play out? Will people be able to obtain the cheer and contentment they are looking for? Will these dogs become family members who share their joie de vivre with their new humans for 10 years or more? We fervently hope so.

We also began to think more about what those searching for a canine family member deserved to gain from this new relationship. What do we all wish for in a dog? We devised this list of the characteristics of an ideal canine family member:

- **Temperament:** Stability, reliability, confidence, trainability, with low risk for aggression to dogs or people
- **Behavioral health:** Ability to fully participate in their human family's lives and activities but can be left at home without objectionable or destructive behavior
- **Physical health and longevity:** Reasonably good day-to-day health without chronic health issues, from allergies to GI issues to orthopedic pain, and to live at least 10 active years
- **Structure:** The anatomy and physiology needed to participate in their families' lives and dog-appropriate activities without pain or discomfort

This last item, canine structure, is an important constellation of physical features of which many people have minimal knowledge. Because dogs have such plastic genetic characteristics, humans can breed dogs, and dogs can interbreed themselves, creating the most structurally varied mammal on earth. Who would

---

*Dr. Gayle Watkins has been breeding Golden Retrievers under the Gaylan's prefix for over 40 years. She has been selected as an AKC Sport Breeder of the Year four times in four different sports. Gayle also founded Avidog International, an online "university" for dog breeders and puppy owners.

believe that the Dachshund and the Irish Wolfhound are not only the same species, but also both bred originally to be hunters?

As a result of this incredible variation in structure, dogs can be comfortable and healthy in their bodies, or not. And that comfort relates directly to temperament, behavior, and physical health. Each one of us has experienced the discomfort of being ill or injured. When we are uncomfortable, we often get irritable, even angry, and sometimes act irrationally. Dogs that are uncomfortable may experience personality changes, including lower thresholds for aggression, decreased interactivity, and increased fear or anxiety.

They certainly are less interested in being trained or joining their humans in activities. Dogs usually recover mentally and behaviorally from short-term discomfort related to an injury but long-term or even lifetime discomfort from disease or structure can affect dogs deeply. Because dogs hide pain and discomfort so well, we may not even recognize it in our own dogs. Often, we perceive the resulting behaviors as flaws in character rather than realizing they have a physical cause. This judgement erodes our relationship. At times, it may even contribute to a dog losing its home.

As a result, it seems imperative that we bring the topic of canine structure to the forefront of our minds and discussions about dogs. It should not just be the purview of breeders who seek to create dogs that win in the conformation ring. Instead, all breeders, whether they breed for conformation, performance, or family dogs, and **all people seeking a new canine companion should be familiar with what constitutes healthy canine structure that provides the physical foundation for temperamentally and behaviorally sound dogs that live active, heathy lives.**

A detailed, accessible study of canine structure and how it affects function has been published by the author and is free to download in full at this link: https://www.frontiersin.org/articles/10.3389/fvets.2020.559055/full. Although this article focuses on the ideal structure for working dogs, the same principles can be applied to defining healthy structure for the family dog.

As more and more of us turn to dogs for comfort and love, let's dig into a conversation about the characteristics required of the consummate canine companion because they work in concert to produce the amazing animal that so many of us want in our lives today.

For references, see Notes, p. 147.

41. The Gift of Being the Only Dog

"Some roads lead on from what you know,
To what you need to find."

--- Della Mae

My very first Golden Retriever, Cajun, was the dog who really got me hooked on canine sports. We competed in obedience, conformation, hunt tests, and the then-new sport of flyball. All that time spent developing a whole new relationship with Cajun through training and competing led to my interest in canine sports medicine and rehabilitation, and the rest, as they say, is history.

When Cajun was older, I had moved to the United States (from Canada) and I had added two more Golden Retrievers to my pack. I had a tiny Toyota that didn't safely fit three Golden Retrievers and all the equipment for competitions, and I couldn't afford a new, larger, vehicle on a post-doctoral fellow's stipend.

Once Cajun had gone as far as he could in competition (there weren't nearly as many dog games available then), I found it necessary to leave him at home while I competed with my other two dogs. After all, dogs just spend all day sleeping, right?

I will never, ever, forget one day as I left the house with my two younger dogs and equipment all packed in the car, and I looked through the window of the door to my house and saw Cajun sitting there, watching me leave. The expression of disappointment on his face brings tears to my eyes even now. I swore I would never do that again.

So, here's to the old guys! And to letting them share fully in our lives for all their lives. And to finding ways that they can be the Only Dog every now and then.

Gifts You Can Give Your Senior Dog

If your dog enjoyed **agility** competition, consider entering them in a competition for exhibition only (FEO) in a lower height class. This allows you to take your past-their-prime agility dog into the ring and do whatever you want. You can take a toy into the ring, play with your oldster, and only do the obstacles you wish, or that your dog will enjoy. Just watch their eyes light up as they remember the old days training and competing.

Another option is to sign your retired pooch up for a novice agility class and jump very low jumps. Who cares if your senior is slower than the other dogs? This is the gift of you spending time together, you and your Only Dog.

And speaking of training – why not teach your old dog some new tricks? How about working on a **tricks title**? The lower levels are easy, and you even get credit if your dog already has a Canine Good Citizen (CGC) title. If you don't already have a CGC, why not make that a goal? With a lifetime of learning under their belt, maybe your oldster will surprise you and earn the higher trick titles. And anyway, it isn't about titles anymore. Your old friend doesn't have anything to prove.

One of the most rewarding experiences for dogs is being able to **use their noses**. Believe it or not, studies have demonstrated that dogs that are given the opportunity to use the ol' schnoz have a more positive outlook on life (Chapter 30). What a gift! Here are two ways you can do this:

1. Food tracking. Go to a park (first thing in the morning is ideal, when there are few other people around) with jillions of slices of mozzarella cheese sticks. (The low-fat ones are best because they are easier to slice, they don't melt much in the heat, and they have fewer calories.) Leave your dog in the car or tied to a post while you find a nice starting point that you'll remember. Put a small pile of mozzarella slices there. Then walk from your starting point to fencepost, to sign, to light standard, keeping mental track of where you went. As you walk, every time you lift your right foot up, drop a piece of mozzarella in the footprint. Then put your dog on a 10- to 12-foot leash and a collar or harness – it doesn't matter which – and take them to the starting point where they can gobble up the pile o' treats. Then guide them to the first mozzarella slice and just follow along as they walk or even run along the food track! See if you can catch a glimpse of the grin on your dog's face, even though you'll be trailing behind.

2. Hide and seek. With your dog in another room, hide mozzarella slices in your house on the floor, in corners, behind small items (turning the ceiling fan on makes it harder), and on elevated places like low shelves, a coffee table, etc. Then release the hound and give lots of encouragement as they search the house for hidden treasure.

3. Coffee break. Take your senior best buddy to a local café. Purchase yourself a favorite drink and request a puppuchino for your canine partner (they're usually free). Sit outside and enjoy the people who will no doubt strike up conversations with you and ask to meet your pal. Dogs are the best social catalyst ever!

If there's no café nearby, grab an ice cream bar for yourself and a Frosty Paws for your frosty-faced friend and head to the local park. Find a bench and meet some new friends. Or if no one's around, enjoy your treat, breathe deeply (because you know that's what your dog is doing), listen to the sounds around you, smell the scents as best you can (because you know that's what your dog is doing), and enjoy all the tiny miracles you can see in the plants or snow or whatever surrounds you. And especially the canine miracle that sits beside you.

I'm sure you can think of lots of other things to do. Take a saunter together, with your dog on a long line, stopping as often as they want. Extra points if you can take your saunter at a big park or a beach. Take your buddy for a swim in a clean lake or a local dog-friendly pool. Just spend some time – any time – letting your senior be the Only Dog for a while.

And as you do that, think about how each canine member of your family has taught you a life lesson, just like Cajun taught me. And be grateful.

An image from the archives. Cajun is the dog on the right (my left).

Notes

Chapter 1. Increase Your Dog's Health & Longevity
Long-term exercise … delays aging:
- Mosole S, Carraro U, Kern H, Loefler S, Fruhmann H, Vogelauer M, Burggraf S, Mayr W, Krenn M, Paternostro-Sluga T, Aram D, Cvecka J, Sedliak M, Tirpakova V, Sarabon N, Musaro A, Sandri M, Protasi F, Nori A, Pold A, Zampieri S. Long-term high-level exercise promotes muscle reinnervation with age. J Neuropathol Exp Neurol 2014;73(4):284-94

younger than to their more sedentary peers:
- Zampieri S, Pietrangelo L, Loefler S, Fruhmann H, Vogelauer M, Burggraf S, Pond A, Grim-Stieger M, Cvecka J, Sedliak M, Tirpakova V, Mayr W, Sarabon N, Rossini K, Barberi L, De Rossi M, Romanello V, Boncompagni S, Musaro A, Sandri M, Protasi F, Carraro U, Kern H. Lifelong physical exercise delays age-associated skeletal muscle decline. J Gerontol A Biol Sci Med Sci 2015;70(2):163-73

achieving a long lifespan:
- Adams VJ, Watson P, Carmichael S, Gerry S, Penell J, Morgan DM. Exceptional longevity and potential determinants of successful ageing in a cohort of 39 Labrador retrievers: results of a prospective longitudinal study. Acta Vet Scand 2016;58(1):29

muscle atrophy that occurs with aging:
- Bowen TS, Schuler G, Adams V. Skeletal muscle wasting in cachexia and sarcopenia: molecular pathophysiology and impact of exercise training. J Cachexia Sarcopenia Muscle 2015; 6(3):197-207
- Montero-Fernandez N, Serra-Rexach JA. Role of exercise on sarcopenia in the elderly. Eur J Phys Rehabil Med 2013;49(1):131-43
- Sembron-tacny A, Dziubek W, Rogowski T, Skorupka E, Dabrowska G. Sarcopenia: monitoring, molecular mechanisms, and physical intervention. Physiol Res 2014;63(6):683-91

responsible for memory and learning:
- van Praag H. Neurogenesis and exercise: past and future directions. Neuromolecular Med. 2008;10(2):128-40
- van Praag H, Christie BR, Sejnowski TJ, Gage FH. Running enhances neurogenesis, learning, and long-term potentiation in mice. Proc Natl Acad Sci USA 1999 Nov 9;96(23):13427-31
- Ahiskot JE, Geda YE, Graff-Radford NR, Petersen RC. Physical exercise as a preventive or disease-modifying treatment of dementia and brain aging. Mayo Clinic Proc 2011;86(9);876-84

Chapter 3. Be Strong!
Strength is directly related to speed:
- Behm DG, Young JD, Whitten JHD, Reid JC, Quigley PJ, Low J, Li Y, Lima CD, Hodgson DD, Chaouachi A, Prieske O, Granacher U. Effectiveness of traditional strength vs. power training on muscle strength, power and speed with youth: A systematic review and meta-analysis. Front Physiol 2017 Jun 30;8:423
- Cronin JB, Hansen KT. Strength and power predictors of sports speed. J Strength Cond Res 2005;19(2):349-57
- Felser S, Behrens M, Fischer S, Heise S, Bäumler M, Salomon R, Bruhn S. Relationship between strength qualities and short track speed skating performance in young athletes. Scand J Med Sci Sports 2016;26(2):165-71

reduce their risk of injuries by 66%:
- Lauersen JB, Andersen TE, Andersen LB. Strength training as superior, dose-dependent and safe prevention of acute and overuse sports injuries: a systematic review, qualitative analysis and meta-analysis. Br J Sports Med 2018;52:1557-1563

Chapter 4. Begging for Answers?
amount of pressure on dogs' articular facets:
- Butterman GR, Schendel MJ, Kahmann RD, Lewis JL, Bradford DS. In vivo facet joint loading of the canine lumbar spine. Spine 1992;17:81-92

Chapter 5. Is Your Dog Hardcore?
the heartache and hassles that accompany these injuries:
- Cullen KL, Dickey JP, Bent LR, Thomason JJ, Moëns NMM. Internet-based survey of the nature and perceived causes of injury to dogs participating in agility training and competition events. J Am Vet Med Assoc 2013;243:1010-1018
- Levy I, Hall C, Trentacosta N, Percival M. A preliminary retrospective survey of injuries occurring in dogs participating in canine agility. Vet Comp Orthop Traumatol 2009;22:321-324

Chapter 6. Let's Not (Static) Stretch…
the effects of stretching in human athletes:
- Behm DG, Blazevich AJ, Kay AD, McHugh M. Acute effects of muscle stretching on physical performance, range of motion, and injury incidence in health active individuals: a systematic review. Appl Physiol Nutr Metab 2016;41:1-11
- Simic L, Sarabon N, Markovic G. Does pre-exercise static stretching inhibit maximal muscular performance? A meta-analytical review. Scand J Med Sci Sports 2013;23:131-148

A meta-analysis examined 125 published studies:
- Behm DG, Blazevich AJ, Kay AD, McHugh M. Acute effects of muscle stretching on physical performance, range of motion, and injury incidence in health active individuals: a systematic review. Appl Physiol Nutr Metab 2016;41:1-11

"involves lengthening a muscle until either a stretch sensation or the point of discomfort is felt":
- Behm DG, Blazevich AJ, Kay AD, McHugh M. Acute effects of muscle stretching on physical performance, range of motion, and injury incidence in health active individuals: a systematic review. Appl Physiol Nutr Metab 2016;41:1-11

"involves the performance of a controlled movement through the range of motion of a joint":
- Behm DG, Blazevich AJ, Kay AD, McHugh M. Acute effects of muscle stretching on physical performance, range of motion, and injury incidence in health active individuals: a systematic review. Appl Physiol Nutr Metab 2016;41:1-11

Chapter 7. Proprioception
reduce the risks of injuries:
- Cadore EL, Rodríguez-Mañas L, Sinclair A, Izquierdo M. Effects of different exercise interventions on risk of falls, gait ability, and balance in physically frail older adults: A systematic review. Rejuvenation Res 2013;16(2):105-114

Chapter 8. Overloaded
one of the major concepts of strength training:
- Rhea MR, Alderman BL. A meta-analysis of periodized versus nonperiodized strength and power training programs. Res Quart Exerc Sport 2004;75(4):413-422

Chapter 10. Reducing Injury Risks
reducing injuries has been published:
- Lauersen JB, Andersen TE, Andersen LB. Strength training as superior, dose-dependent and safe prevention of acute and overuse sports injuries: a systematic review, qualitative analysis and meta-analysis. Br J Sports Med 2018;52:1557-1563

both strength and proprioceptive exercises reduce injury risk:
- Lauersen JB, Bertelsen DM, Andersen LB. The effectiveness of exercise interventions to prevent sports injuries: a systematic review and meta-analysis of randomized controlled trials.

Br J Sports Med 2014; 48(11): 871-7

proprioceptive exercises reduce the risk of injury:
- Riva D, Bianchi R, Roc ca F, Mamo C. Proprioception training and injury prevention in a professional men's basketball team: A six-year prospective study. J Strength Cond Res 2016; 30(2): 461-75

A brain study was undertaken:
- Diekfuss JA, Grooms DR, Yuan W, Dudley J, Barber Foss KD, Thomas S, Ellis JD, Schneider DK, Leach J, Bonnette S, Myer GD. Does brain functional connectivity contribute to musculoskeletal injury? A preliminary prospective analysis of a neural biomarker of ACL injury risk. J Sci Med Sport 2019;22(2):169-174

Chapter 11. Stop Taking Your Dog for a Walk!

science of strength training for humans is very clear:
- Suchomel TJ, Nimphius S, Bellon CR, Stone MH. The importance of muscular strength: Training considerations. Sports Med 2018;48:765-785

increases the likelihood that you will exercise:
- Christian H, Bauman A, Epping JN, Levine GN, McCormack G, Rhodes RE, Richards E, Rock M, Westgarth C. Encouraging dog walking for health promotion and disease prevention. Analytic review. Amer J Lifestyle Med 2016;12(3):233-243

got more and better sleep than non-dog owners:
- Mičková E, Machová K, Daďová K, Svobodová I. Does dog ownership affect physical activity, sleep, and self-reported health in older adults? Int J Environ Res Public Health 2019; 16:3355

Chapter 12. Play Ball!...Safely

provide deep joy, contentment, and optimism to many dogs:
- Coppinger R , Coppinger L. Dogs. A New Understanding of Canine Origin, Behavior and Evolution. University of Chicago Press 2001. Chapter 6. Behavioral Conformation. pp 189-224

Chapter 13. No Hot Dogs Please!

temperature or humidity in contributing to heatstroke:
- Bruchim Y, Klement E, Saragusty J, Finkeilstein E, Kass P, Aroch I. Heatstroke in dogs: A retrospective study of 54 cases (1999-2004) and analysis of risk factors for death. J Vet Med 2006;20:38-46

very uncomfortable when it is above 28:
- Bruchim Y, Klement E, Saragusty J, Finkeilstein E, Kass P, Aroch I. Heatstroke in dogs: A retrospective study of 54 cases (1999-2004) and analysis of risk factors for death. J Vet Med 2006;20:38-46

the mouth, nasal passages, pharynx, larynx, etc.:
- Dickerson AK, Mills ZG, Hu DL. Wet mammals shake at tuned frequencies to dry. J R Soc Interface 2012;9:3208-3218

region in the genome that was associated with heat tolerance:
- Huson HJ, vonHoldt BM, Rimbault M, Byers AM, Runstadler JA, Parker HG, Ostrander EA. Breed-specific ancestry studies and genome-wide association analysis highlight an association between the MYH9 gene and heat tolerance in Alaskan sprint racing sled dogs. Mamm Genome 2012;23:178-194

shown to have poorer cooling mechanisms:
- Davis MS, Cummings SL, Payton ME. Effect of brachycephaly and body condition score on respiratory thermoregulation of healthy dogs. J Am Vet Med Assoc 2017;251:1160-1165

region in the genome that was associated with heat tolerance:
- Huson HJ, vonHoldt BM, Rimbault M, Byers AM, Runstadler JA, Parker HG, Ostrander EA.

Breed-specific ancestry studies and genome-wide association analysis highlight an association between the MYH9 gene and heat tolerance in Alaskan sprint racing sled dogs. Mamm Genome 2012;23:178-194

shown to have poorer cooling mechanisms:
- Davis MS, Cummings SL, Payton ME. Effect of brachycephaly and body condition score on respiratory thermoregulation of healthy dogs. J Am Vet Med Assoc 2017;251:1160-1165

more likely to die if they do experience heatstroke:
- Bruchim Y, Klement E, Saragusty J, Finkeilstein E, Kass P, Aroch I. Heatstroke in dogs: A retrospective study of 54 cases (1999-2004) and analysis of risk factors for death. J Vet Med 2006;20:38-46

three mechanisms for cooling dogs after a 15-min treadmill exercise:
- Davis MS, Marcellin-Little DJ, O'Connor E. Comparison of postexercise cooling methods in working dogs. J Spec Oper med 2019;19(1):56-60

Chapter 14. Star Light, Star Bright
the form of energy that the cell uses for healing:
- Passarella S, Casamassima E, Molinari S, Pastore D, Quagliariello E, Catalano IM, Cingolani A. Increase of proton electrochemical potential and ATP synthesis in rat liver mitochondria irradiated in vitro by helium-neon laser. FEBS Let 1984;175:95-99

PBMT can promote tissue regeneration, reduce inflammation and relieve pain:
- Alves AN, Fernandes KP, Deana AM, Bussadori SK, Mesquita-Ferrari RA Effects of low-level laser therapy on skeletal muscle repair: a systematic review. Am J Phys Med Rehabil 2014; 93(12):1073-85

stroke, traumatic brain injury, Parkinson's disease, and depression:
- Rojas JC, Gonzalez-Lima F. Neurological and psychological applications of transcranial lasers and LEDs. Biochemical Pharmacology 2013; 86:447–457

effects of PBMT on human sports performance:
- Ferraresi C, Huang Y-Y, Hamblin MR. Photobiomodulation in human muscle tissue: an advantage in sports performance? J Biophotonics 2016;9(11-12):1273-1299

effects of PBMT on the performance of high-level rugby players:
- Pinto HD, Vanin AA, Miranda EF, Tomazoni SS, Johnson DS, Albuquerque-Pontes GM, Alexio Junior I de O, Grandinetti V dos S, Casalechi HL, de Carvalho P de TC, Leal-Junior ECP. Photobiomodulation therapy improves performance and accelerates recovery of high-level rugby players in field test: A randomized, crossover, double-blind, placebo-controlled clinical study. J Strength Cond Res 2016;30(12):3329-3338

higher doses can have no effect or might, in fact, be harmful:
- Rojas JC, Gonzalez-Lima F. Neurological and psychological applications of transcranial lasers and LEDs. Biochemical Pharmacology 2013; 86:447–457
- Ferraresi C, Huang Y-Y, Hamblin MR. Photobiomodulation in human muscle tissue: an advantage in sports performance? J Biophotonics 2016;9(11-12):1273-1299

penetration of laser light through fur:
- Laakso L, Richardson C, Cramond T. Factors affecting low level laser therapy. Aust J Physiother 1993;39(2):95-9

the darker the skin, the less the light penetrates to the tissues below:
- Souza-Barros L, Dhaidan G, Maunula M, Solomon V, Gabison D, Lilge L, Nussbaum EL. Skin color and tissue thickness effects on transmittance, reflectance, and skin temperature when using 635 and 808 nm lasers in low intensity therapeutics. Lasers Surg Med 2018;50:291-301

should be placed on the World Anti-Doping Agency's list of prohibited substances:
- Ferraresi C, Huang Y-Y, Hamblin MR. Photobiomodulation in human muscle tissue: an

advantage in sports performance? J Biophotonics 2016;9(11-12):1273-1299

Chapter 15. Do the Dewclaws?
put the toes at risk for injuries:
- Sellon DC, Martucci K, Wenz JR, Marcellin-Little DJ, Powers M, Cullen KL. A survey of risk factors for digit injuries among dogs training and competing in agility events. J Am Vet Med Assoc 2018;252:75–83

Chapter 16. Digit Injuries
to identify potential risk factors for digit injuries in these dogs:
- Sellon DC, Martucci K, Wenz JR, Marcellin-Little DJ, Powers M, Cullen KL. A survey of risk factors for digit injuries among dogs training and competing in agility events. J Am Vet Med Assoc 2018;252:75–83

Chapter 17. A-Frame-Induced Carpal Injuries?
A-frame might contribute to agility-related injuries:
- Levy M, Hall C, Trentacosta N, Percival M. A preliminary retrospective survey of injuries occurring in dogs participating in canine agility. Vet Comp Orthop Traumatol 2009;22(04):321–324
- Cullen KL, Dickey JP, Bent LR, Thomason JJ, Moëns NM. Internet-based survey of the nature and perceived causes of injury to dogs participating in agility training and competition events. J Am Vet Med Assoc 2013;243(07):1010–1018

the angle of the carpal (wrist) joint:
- Appelgrein C, Glyde MR, Hosgood G, Dempsey AR, Wickham S. Reduction of the A-frame angle of incline does not change the maximum carpal joint extension angle in agility dogs entering the A-frame. Vet Comp Orthop Traumatol 2018;31:77-82

maximal carpal angles for Beagles of 49.2 degrees:
- Lorke M, Willen M, Lucas K, Beyerbach M, Wefstaedt P, Murua Escobar H, Nolte I. Comparative kinematic gait analysis in young and old Beagle dogs. J Vet Sci 2017;18(4):521-530
- Agostinho FS, Rahal SC, Miqueleto ML, Vergugo MR, Inamassu LR, El-Warrak AO. Kinematic analysis of Labrador Retrievers and Rottweilers trotting on a treadmill. Vet Comp Orthop Traumatol 2011;24:185-191

Chapter 19. My Dog in Rehab Needs Stuff to Do
long-term crate rest causes significant muscle atrophy:
- Sneddon, JC, Minnaar, PP, Grosskopf, JF, Groeneveld, HT. Physiological and blood biochemical responses to submaximal treadmill exercise in Canaan dogs before, during and after training. J S Afr Vet Assoc 1989;60:87–91

Chapter 20. The Genetics of Athletic Success
A fascinating study, compared whole-genome DNA sequence data:
- Sneddon, JC, Minnaar, PP, Kim J, Williams FJ, Dreger DL, Plassais J, Davis BW, Parker HG, Ostrander EA. Genetic selection of athletic success in sport-hunting dogs. PNAS 2018;115(30):E7212-E7221

Chapter 21. Telomeres and Your Dog's Lifespan
dogs with longer telomeres live longer:
- Fick LJ, Fick GH, Li Z, Cao E, Bao Bo, Heffelfinger D, Parker HG, Ostrander EA, and Riabowo K. Telomere length correlates with life span of dog breeds. Cell Reports 2012;2:1530–1536

mortality data from a meta-analysis of 74,556 dogs:
- Fleming JM, Creevy KE, and Promislow DE. (2011). Mortality in North American dogs from

1984 to 2004: an investigation into age-, size-, and breed-related causes of death. J Vet Intern Med 2011;25:187–198

multiplies its weight approximately 112 times to reach adult size:
- Groppetti D, Pecile A, Palestrini C, Marelli SP and Boracchi P. A national census of birth weight in purebred dogs in Italy. Animals 2017;7:43

physical activity, a diet rich in **fresh food** and **antioxidants**:
- Arsenis NC, You T, Ogawa EF, Tinsley GM, Zuo L. Physical activity and telomere length: Impact of aging and potential mechanisms of action. Oncotarget 2017;8(27):45008-45019
- Tucker LA. Physical activity and telomere length in US men and women: An NHANES investigation. Prevent Med 2017;100:145-151
- Xu Q, Parks CG, DeRoo LA, Cawthon RM, Dale P Sandler DP, and Chen H. Multivitamin use and telomere length in women. Am J Clin Nutr 2009;89:1857–63
- Garcia-Calzon S, Moleres A, Martinez-Gonzales MA, Martinez JA, Zalba G, Marti A, GENOI Members. Dietary total antioxidant capacity is associated with leukocyte telomere length in a children and adolescent population. Clinical Nutrition 2017;34:694e699
- Epel ES, Blackburn EH, Lin J, Dhabhar FS, Adler NE, Morrow JD and Cawthorn RM. Accelerated telomere shortening in response to life stress. PNAS 2004;101: 17312–17315

offspring conceived by older fathers have longer telomeres:
- Eisenberg DTA, Kuzawa CW. Commentary: The evolutionary biology of the paternal age effect on telomere length. Int J Epid 2013;42(2):462p465

Chapter 22. No Weigh!

People who are overweight have an **increased risk of cancer** and **other systemic diseases:**
- Cowey S, Hardy RW. The metabolic syndrome: A high-risk state for cancer? Am J Pathol 2006;169:1505–1522
- Martin LJ, Siliart B, Dumon HJ, Nguyen, PG. Hormonal disturbances associated with obesity in dogs. J Anim Physiol Anim Nutr (Berl) 2006;90:355–360
- Bach JF, Rozanski, EA, Bedenice D, Chan DL, Freeman LM, Lofgren JL, Oura TJ, Hoffman AM. Association of expiratory airway dysfunction with marked obesity in healthy adult dogs. Am J Vet Res 2007;68:670–675
- Zou C, Shao J. 2008. Role of adipocytokines in obesity-associated insulin resistance. J Nutr Biochem 2008;19:277–286

Dogs kept a normal weight live longer:
- Salt C, Morris PJ, Wilson D, Lund EM, German AJ. Association between life span and body condition in neutered client-owned dogs. J Vet Intern Med 2019;33:89–99

slightly lean body condition has been shown to **decrease the risk of osteoarthritis:**
- Budsberg SC, Bartges JW. Nutrition and osteoarthritis in dogs: does it help? Vet Clin North Am Small Anim Pract 2006;36(6):1307–1323

Chapter 23. How to Make Your Dog Live Longer
lifespans of over 50,000 dogs of 12 different breeds:
- Salt C, Morris PJ, Wilson D, Lund EM, German AJ. Association between life span and body condition in neutered client-owned dogs. J Vet Intern Med 2019;33:89–99

gain weight unless their food intake is carefully monitored:
- de Godoy MRC. Pancosma Comparative Gut Physiology Symposium: All About Appetite Regulation: Effects of diet and gonadal steroids on appetite regulation and food intake of companion animals. J Anim Sci 2018;96(8):3526–3536

examining lifespan in a colony of overweight vs normal weight Labrador Retrievers:
- Kealy RD, Lawler DF, Ballam JM, Mantz SL, Biery DN, Greeley EH, Lust G, Segre M, Smith GK, Stoew HD. Effects of diet restriction on life span and age-related changes in dogs. J Am Vet Med Assoc 2002;220:1315-1320

Discovering the Dog
The Gift of Being the Only Dog

Increased prevalence of fatal cancers in spayed and neutered large breed dogs:
- Torres de la Riva g, Hart BL, Farver TB, Oberbauer AM, Messam LL McV, Willis N, Hart LA. Neutering dogs: Effects on joint disorders and cancers in Golden Retrievers. PLoS ONE 2013;8:e55937
- Hart BL, Hart LA, Thigpen AP, Willits NH. Long-term health effects of neutering dogs: Comparison of Labrador Retrievers with Golden Retrievers. PLoS ONE 2014;9:e102241
- Zink MC, Farhoody P, Elser SE, Ruffini LD, Gibbons TA, Rieger RH. Evaluation of the risk and age of onset of cancer and behavioral disorders in gonadectomized Vizslas. J Am Vet Med Assoc 2014;244:309-319
- Hart BL, Hart LA, Thigpen AP, Willits NH. Neutering of German Shepherd Dogs: Associated joint disorders, cancers and urinary incontinence. Vet Med Sci 2016;2(3):191–199

Dogs that are overweight are more susceptible to a variety of chronic conditions:
- German AJ, Ryan VH, German AC, Wood IS, Trayhurn P. Obesity, its associated disorders and the role of inflammatory adipokines in companion animals. Vet J 2010;185:4-9
- Lund EM, Armstrong PJ, Kirk CA, Klausner JS. Prevalence and risk factors for obesity in adult dogs from private US veterinary practices. Int J Appl Res Vet Med 2006;4:177-186
- German AJ, Hervera M, Hunter L, Holden SL, Morris PJ, Biourge V, Trayhurn P. Improvement in insulin resistance and reduction in plasma inflammatory adipokines after weight loss in obese dogs. Domest Anim Endocrinol 2009;37:214-226
- Tvarijonaviciute A, Ceron JJ, Holden SL, Cuthbertson DJ, Biourge V, Morris PJ, German AJ. Obesity-related metabolic dysfunction in dogs: a comparison with human metabolic syndrome. BMC Vet Res 2012;8:147
- Tvarijonaviciute A, Ceron JJ, Holden SL, Biourge V, Morris PJ, German AJ. Effect of weight loss in obese dogs on indicators of renal function or disease. J Vet Intern Med 2013;27:31-38
- Mosing M, German AJ, Holden SL, MacFarlane P, Biourge V, Morris PJ, Iff I. Oxygenation and ventilation characteristics in obese sedated dogs before and after weight loss: a clinical trial. Vet J 2013;198:367-371
- German AJ, Holden SL, Wiseman-Orr ML, Reid J, Nolan AM, Biourge V, Morris PJ Scott EM. Quality of life is reduced in obese dogs but improves after successful weight loss. Vet J 2012;192: 428-434

financial impact of having an obese dog was estimated to be approximately $2000 a year:
- Bomberg E, Birch L, Endenburg E, German AH, Neilson J, Seligman H, Takashima G, Day MJ. The financial costs, behaviour and psychology of obesity: A one health analysis. J Comp Pathol 2017; 156:310-325

Chapter 24. Inflammatory Food?
dietary fat was the major nutritional cause of heart disease:
- Kearns CE, Schmidt LA, Glantz SA. Sugar industry and coronary heart disease research: A historical analysis of internal industry documents. JAMA Intern Med 2016;176(11):1680–1685

kibble contains between 46 and 74% carbohydrates:
- National Research Council, National Academy of Science. Nutrient Requirements of Dogs and Cats, 2006 Edition. National Academies Press, Washington, DC, p 317

Percent carbohydrates required by adult dogs to sustain life: zero:
- National Research Council, National Academy of Science. Nutrient Requirements of Dogs and Cats, 2006 Edition. National Academies Press, Washington, DC, p 317

the superheating process during the production of kibble changes the quality of some nutrients:
- Teodorowicz M, Hendriks WH, Wichers HJ, Savelkoul HFJ. Immunomodulation by processed animal feed: The role of Maillard reaction products and advanced glycation end-products (AGEs). Frontiers in Immunology 2018;9:2088

a series of chemical rearrangements occurs, called the Maillard reaction:
- Hodge JE. Chemistry of browning reactions in model systems. J Agric Food Chem

1953;1:928-43

decreases the availability of certain amino acids in the dog's food:
- Teodorowicz M, Hendriks WH, Wichers HJ, Savelkoul HFJ. Immunomodulation by processed animal feed: The role of Maillard reaction products and advanced glycation end-products (AGEs). Frontiers in Immunology 2018;9:2088

they accumulate and gradually become part of the protein structure of the entire body:
- John WG, Lamb BJ. The maillard or browning reaction in diabetes. Eye 1993;7:230-7

development of **cancers** in both humans and dogs:
- Ramasay R, Vannucci J, Yan D, Herold K, Yan F, Schmidt AM. Advanced glycation end products and RAGE: a common thread in aging, diabetes, neurodegeneration, and inflammation. Glycobiology 2005;15:16-28R
- Gentzel JB. Does contemporary canine diet cause cancer? A review. Vet World 2013;6:532-9

AGEs can hinder the **repair** of tissues:
- Gentzel JB. Does contemporary canine diet cause cancer? A review. Vet World 2013;6:532-9.
- Vlassara H, Bucala R, Striker LJ. Pathogenic effects of advanced glycosylation: biochemical, biologic and clinical implications for diabetes and aging. Lab Invest 1994;70:138-51

linked to atherosclerosis, kidney disease, retinopathy, osteoarthritis, neurodegenerative diseases and diabetes mellitus:
- Teodorowicz M, Hendriks WH, Wichers HJ, Savelkoul HFJ. Immunomodulation by processed animal feed: The role of Maillard reaction products and advanced glycation end-products (AGEs). Frontiers in Immunology 2018;9:2088

detected in tissues of people with **diabetes, cataracts, osteoarthritis, canine cognitive dysfunction syndrome**, **vascular dysfunction**, and **atherosclerosis**:
- Teodorowicz M, Hendriks WH, Wichers HJ, Savelkoul HFJ. Immunomodulation by processed animal feed: The role of Maillard reaction products and advanced glycation end-products (AGEs). Frontiers in Immunology 2018;9:2088

increase in allergic responses in the gut, expressed as **inflammatory bowel disease:**
- Teodorowicz M, Hendriks WH, Wichers HJ, Savelkoul HFJ. Immunomodulation by processed animal feed: The role of Maillard reaction products and advanced glycation end-products (AGEs). Frontiers in Immunology 2018;9:2088

AGE levels in canned food are higher than kibble:
- van Rooijen C, Bosch G, van der Poel AF, Wierenga PA, Alexander L, Hendriks WH. Quantitation of Maillard reaction products in commercially available pet foods. J Agric Food Chem 2014;62:8883-91
- Crissey SD, Swanson JA, Lintzenich BA, Brewer BA, Slifka KA. Use of a raw meat-based diet or a dry kibble for sand cats (*Felis margarita*). J Anim Sci 1997;75:2154-2160

average daily intake by most dogs is 122 times higher than that of humans:
- van Rooijen C, Bosch G, van der Poel AF, Wierenga PA, Alexander L, Hendriks WH. Quantitation of Maillard reaction products in commercially available pet foods. J Agric Food Chem 2014;62:8883-91

Chapter 25. Smart Supplementation
Vitamins and minerals in their natural, fresh forms often have better bioavailability:
- Rey AI, Segura J, Olivares A, Cerisuelo A, Piñero C, López-Bote CJ. Effect of micellized natural (D-α-tocopherol) vs. synthetic (DL-α-tocopheryl acetate) vitamin E supplementation given to turkeys on oxidative status and breast meat quality characteristics. Poult Sci 2015;94(6):1259-1269

strong evidence for the systemic anti-inflammatory effects of omega-3 fatty acid:
- Lu X, Machado GC, Eyles JP, Ravi V, Hunter DJ. Dietary supplements for treating osteoarthritis: a systematic review and meta-analysis. J Sports Med 2018 Feb;52(3):167-175

- Ticinesi A, Meschi T, Laurentani F, Felis G, Franchi F, Pedrolli C, Barichella M, Benati G, Di Nuzzo S, Ceda GP, Maggio M. Nutrition and inflammation in older individuals: Focus on vitamin D, polyunsaturated fatty acids and whey proteins. Nutrients 2016 Mar 29;8(4):186

improve inflammatory bowel disease, and boost responses to vaccines:
- Craig, JM. Atopic dermatitis and the intestinal microbiota in humans and dogs. J Vet Med Sci 2016; 2 (2):95-105
- Benyacoub J, GL Czarnecki-Maulden, Cavadini C, Sauthier T, Anderson RE, Schiffrin EJ, von der Weid T. Supplementation of food with Enterococcus faecium (SF68) stimulates immune functions in young dogs. J Nutr 2003;133(4):1158–1162
- Rossi G, G Pengo, Caldin M, Piccionello AP, Steiner JM, Cohen ND, Jergens AE, Suchodolski JS. Comparison of microbiological, histological, and immunomodulatory parameters in response to treatment with either combination therapy with prednisone and metronidazole or probiotic VSL#3 strains in dogs with idiopathic inflammatory bowel disease PLoS One 2014 Apr 10;9(4):e94699

there was also a need for higher quality evidence:
- Rey AI, Segura J, Olivares A, Cerisuelo A, Piñero C, López-Bote CJ. Effect of micellized natural (D-α-tocopherol) vs. synthetic (DL-α-tocopheryl acetate) vitamin E supplementation given to turkeys on oxidative status and breast meat quality characteristics. Poult Sci 2015;94(6):1259-1269

diets containing antioxidants improved cognitive function in old dogs:
- Pan Y, AD Kennedy Jönsson T, Milgram NW. Cognitive enhancement in old dogs from dietary supplementation with a nutrient blend containing arginine, antioxidants, B vitamins and fish oil. Br J Nutr 2018 Feb;119(3):349-358
- Christie LA, WO Opii, Head E. Strategies for improving cognition with aging: insights from a longitudinal study of antioxidant and behavioral enrichment in canines. *Age (Dordr)* 2009 Sep; 31(3):211–220

vegetables may prevent or slow progression of cancer in dogs:
- Raghavan M, Knapp DW, Bonney PL, Dawson MH, Glickman LT. Evaluation of the effect of dietary vegetable consumption on reducing risk of transitional cell carcinoma of the urinary bladder in Scottish Terriers. J Am Vet Med Assoc 2005;227(1):94-100

Chapter 26. Yeast – Yuck!
it creates an imbalance in the body's homeostasis; the fungus itself is quite immunogenic :
- Bond R, Morris DO, Guillot J, Bensignor EJ, Robson D, Mason KV, Kano R, Hill PB. Biology, diagnosis and treatment of *Malassezia* dermatitis in dogs and cats. Clinical consensus guidelines of the World Association for Veterinary Dermatology. Vet Dermatol 2020;31:27-e4

Chapter 27. The Cure in Curcumin
87% of all injuries involved soft tissues:
- Cullen KL, Dickey JP, Bent LR, Thomason JJ, Moens NMM. Internet-based survey of the nature and perceived causes of injury to dogs participating in agility training and competition events. J Am Vet Med Assoc 2013;243:1010-1018

an even higher proportion of active and older dogs:
- Fleming JM, Creevy KE, Promislow DEL. Mortality in North American dogs from 1984 to 2004: An investigation into age-, size- and breed-related causes of death. J Vet Intern Med 2011:25:187-198

chronic inflammatory illnesses such as neurodegenerative, cardiovascular, neoplastic, pulmonary, metabolic, and autoimmune diseases:
- Aggarwal BB. Harikumar K. Potential therapeutic effects of curcumin, the anti-inflammatory agent, against neurodegenerative, cardiovascular, pulmonary, metabolic, autoimmune and neoplastic diseases. Int J Biochem Cell Biol 2009;41:40–59

effects of curcumin on the healing of tendons in rats:
- Jiang D, Gao P, Lin H, Geng H. Curcumin improves tendon healing in rats: a histological, biochemical, and functional evaluation. Connect Tissue Res 2016;57(1):20-7

treated either with curcumin or a nonsteroidal anti-inflammatory drug:
- Colitti M, Gaspardo B, Della Pria A, Scaini C, Stefanon B. Transcriptome modification of white blood cells after dietary administration of curcumin and non-steroidal anti-inflammatory drug in osteoarthritic affected dogs. Vet Immunol Immunopathol 2012;147:136-146

Chapter 28. To Harness or Not to Harness?

effect of restrictive and non-restrictive harnesses on shoulder extension in dogs when walking and trotting:
- Lafuente MP, Provis L, Schmalz EA. Effects of restrictive and non-restrictive harnesses on shoulder extension in dogs at walk and trot. Vet Record 2018;1-7

A previous harness study did look at those parameters:
- Carr BJ, Dresse K, Zink MC. The effects of five commercially available harnesses on canine gait. Proceedings of ACVS Surgical Summit, 2016

discussed in an excellent book by Turid Rugaas:
- Rugaas T. My Dog Pulls. What Do I Do? 2005, Dogwise Publishing

Chapter 29. Love, Actually

Oxytocin makes you feel good when you're with someone you love by stimulating the reward center in your brain, and it also reduces stress:
- Dölen G, Darvishzadeh A, Huang KW, Malenka RC. Social reward requires coordinated activity of nucleus accumbens oxytocin and serotonin. Nature 2013;501(7466):179-84
- Neumann ID. Involvement of the brain oxytocin system in stress coping: interactions with the hypothalamo-pituitary-adrenal axis. Prog Brain Res 2002;139:147-62

oxytocin release into the blood stream of both species:
- Odendaal JS, Meintjes RA. Neurophysiological correlates of affiliative behaviour between humans and dogs Vet J 2003;165(3):296-301

before and after spending 30 minutes in a room together:
- Nagasawa M, Mitsui S, En S, Ohtani N, Obta M, Sakuma Y, Onaka T, Mogi K, Kikusui T. Oxytocin-gaze positive loop and the coevolution of human-dog bonds. Science 2015;348(6232): 333-336

Chapter 30. How to Make Your Dog More Optimistic

expect more negative outcomes than rats living in predictable conditions:
- Harding EJ, Paul ES, Mendl M. Cognitive bias and affective state. Nature 2004;427:312

Sheep that are released from restraint develop a more positive cognitive bias:
- Doyle RE, Fisher A, Hinch GN, Biossy A, Lee C. Release from restraint generates a positive judgment bias in sheep. Appl Anim Behav Sci 2010;122:28-34

more optimistic than pigs in a less enriched environment:
- Asher L, Friel M, Griffin K, Collins LM. Mood and personality interact to determine cognitive biases in pigs. Biology Letters 2016;12:20160402

a liquid containing less sugar as compared to bees from a stable hive:
- Bateson M, Desire S, Gartside SE, Wright GA. Agitated honeybees exhibit pessimistic cognitive biases. Current Biology 2011;21(12):1070-1073

the dog is observed to see how many seconds it takes to approach the bowl:
- Bethell EJ. A "how-to" guide for designing judgment bias studies to assess captive animal welfare. J Appl Anim Wel Sci 2015;18(sup1):S18-S42

compare the attitude of dogs that had been trained in nosework or heeling:
- Duranton C, Horowitz A. Let me sniff! Nosework induces positive judgment bias in pet dogs. Appl Anim Behav Sci 2019;211:61-66

Oxytocin also improves cognitive bias in dogs:
- Kis A, Hernadi A, Kanizsar O, Gacsi M, Topal J. Oxytocin induces positive expectations about ambivalent stimuli (cognitive bias) in dogs. Hormone Behav 2015;69:1-7

Chapter 31. Scents of Success

scent sensitivity compared to physically conditioned dogs:
- Angle CT, Wakshlag JJ, Gillette RL, Steury T, Haney P, Barrett J, Fischer T. The effects of exercise and diet on olfactory capability in detection dogs. *J Nutr Sci* 2014;3:e44

higher frequency of correct target alerts in physically fit dogs:
- Gazit I, Terkel J. Explosives detection by sniffer dogs following strenuous physical activity. Appl Anim Behav Sci 2003;81:149-61

exercised dogs maintained their olfactory acuity:
- Altom EK, Davenport GM, Myers LJ, Cummins KA. Effect of dietary fat source and exercise on odorant-detecting ability of canine athletes. Research in Veterinary Science 2003;75:149–155

searched more accurately 30 min following the consumption of breakfast than when fasted:
- Miller HC, Bender C. The breakfast effect: Dogs (*Canis familiaris*) search more accurately when they are less hungry. Behav Proc 2012;91:313-317

contribute to reduced odor detection ability:
- Andress M, Goodnight ME. Heatstroke in a military working dog. US Army Med Dep J 2013;1: 34-7

dehydration can significantly decrease odor detection capabilities in dogs:
- Altom EK, Davenport GM, Myers LJ, Cummins KA. Effect of dietary fat source and exercise on odorant-detecting ability of canine athletes. Research in Veterinary Science 2003;75:149–155

Older dogs can have age-related changes in their scenting system:
- Hirai T, Kojima S, Shimada A. Age-related changes in the olfactory system of dogs. Neuropathol Appl Neurobiol 1996;22(6):532-9

list of pharmaceuticals that can cause reduced scenting ability in humans:
- Bromley SM. Smell and taste disorders: a primary care approach. Am Fam Physician 2000;61: 427-36
- McNeill EJM, Carrie S. Olfactory dysfunction – assessment and management J ENT Masterclass 2009;2:68-73
- Scott AE. Clinical characteristics of taste and smell disorders. Ear Nose Throat J 1989;68:297-298,301,304-21

high doses of metronidazole, steroids, and chemotherapeutics:
- Jenkins EK, Lee-Fowler TM, Angle TC, Behrend EN, Moore GE. Effects of oral administration of metronidazole and doxycycline on olfactory capabilities of explosives detection dogs. Am J Vet Res 2016;77:906-12

hypothyroidism, diabetes, and Cushing's disease can reduce scenting ability in dogs:
- Dysosmia of the dog in clinical veterinary medicine. Prog Vet Neurol 1990;1:171-9 199:1093-1104

differences of as little as 1/1000 of a degree:
- Bakken GS, Colayori SE, Duong T. Analytical methods for the geometric optics of thermal vision illustrated with four species of pit vipers. Exp. Biol 2012;215:2621-2629

get a food reward if they pushed a sliding panel that was very slightly warm:
- Bálint A, Andics A, Gácsi M, Gábor A, Czeibert K, Luce CM, Miklósi A, Kröger RHH. Dogs can sense weak thermal radiation. Scientific Reports Nature Research 2020;10:3736

the black fire beetle, certain snake species, and … the vampire bat:
- Hammer DX, Schmitz H, Schmitz A, Rylander A, Welch AJ. Sensitivity threshold and response characteristics of infrared detection in the beetle *Melanophila acuminate* (Coleoptera: Buprestidae). Comp Biochem Physiol Part A Mol Integr Physiol 2001;128:805–819
- Goris R C. Infrared organs of snakes: An integral part of vision. J Herpetol 2011;45:2–14Kürten L, Schmidt U. Thermoperception in the common vampire bat (*Desmodus rotundus*). J Comp Physiol 1982;146:223–228

Chapter 32. Cold Nose, Warm Sense

sides of their faces that are moist and colder than the snake's skin:
- Cadena V, Andrade D, Bovo RP, Tattersall G J. Evaporative respiratory cooling augments pit organ thermal detection in rattlesnakes. J Comp Physiol A Sens Neural Behav Physiol 2013;

people pay attention to the same area when looking at pictures of dogs:
- Guo K, Tunnicliffe D, Roebuck H. Human spontaneous gaze patterns in viewing of faces of different species. Perception 2010;39:533-542

when humans lift their inner eyebrows, it makes them seem sad:
- Ekman P, Friesen WV, Hager JC. Facial Action Coding System: The Manual. Network Information Research, Salt Lake City, UT, 2002

attracted to large eyes, like human babies have:
- Archer J, Monton S. Preferences for infant facial features in pet dogs and cats. Ethology 2011;117:217-226

animals that have visible sclera (the whites of the eye):
- Segal NL, Goetz AT, Maldonado AC. Preferences for visible white sclera in adults, children and autism spectrum disorder children: Implications of the cooperative eye hypothesis. Evol Hum Behav 2016;37:35-39

dogs with this sad-eyed appearance were more likely to be rehomed from shelters:
- Waller BM, Peirce K, Caeiro CC, Scheider L, Burrows AM, McCune S, Kaminski J. Paedomorphic facial expressions give dogs a selective advantage. PLoS One 2013;8(12):e82686

Chapter 33. On the One Hand…

activates "fight or flight" responses:
- Siniscalchi M, d'Ingeo S, Quaranta A. Lateralized functions in the dog brain. Symmetry 2017;9:71

judge whether a dog is right-pawed or left-pawed:
- Tomkins LM, Thomson PC, McGreevy PD. First-stepping test as a measure of motor laterality in dogs (*Canis familiaris*). J Vet Behav 2010;5:247-255

the right brain was responding to the arousing stimulus:
- Siniscalchi M, d'Ingeo S, Quaranta A. Lateralized functions in the dog brain. Symmetry 2017;9:71

turned their heads to the left suggesting an alarm-based response:
- Branson NJ, Rogers LJ. Relationship between paw preference strength and nose phobia in Canis familiaris J Comp Psychol 2006;120:176-183

relaxed in unfamiliar environments and when presented with novel stimuli:
- Tomkins LM, Thomson PC, McGreevy PD. Associations between motor, sensory and structural lateralization and guide dog success. Vet J 2012;192:359-367

the dogs again wagged their tails more to the right:
- Quaranta, A.; Siniscalchi, M.; Vallortigara, G. Asymmetric tail-wagging responses by dogs to different emotive stimuli. Curr Biol 2007, 17, R199–R201

Chapter 34. The Eyes Have It
the muscles around the eyes, of dogs and wolves:
- Kaminski J, Waller BM, Diogo R, Hartstone-Rose A, Burrows AM. The evolution of facial muscle anatomy in dogs. PNAS 2019;116(29):14677-14681

establish eye contact with humans when they cannot solve a problem:
- Archer J, Monton S. Preferences for infant facial features in pet dogs and cats. Ethology 2011;117:217-226

to emphasize certain words or phrases:
- Guaïtella I, Santi S, Lagrue B, Cáve C. Are eyebrow movements linked to voice variations and turn-taking in dialogue? An experimental investigation. Lang Speech 2009;52:207-222

tend to focus on the upper facial area, and particularly the eyes:
- Krahmer W, Ruttka Z, Swerts M, Wellelink W. Pitch, eyebrows and the perception of focus. *In*. B. Bel, I Marliens. Eds. Speech Prosody 2002. pp. 443-446

Chapter 35. Be-Yawn Compare
neural networks responsible for empathy and social skills are activated:
- Nahab FB, Hattori N, Saad ZS, Hallett M. Contagious yawning and the frontal lobe: an fMRI study. Hum Brain Mapp 2009;30:1744–1751

people who score higher on self-recognition ... are more susceptible to yawn contagiously:
- Platek SM, Critton SR, Myers TEJ, Gallup GG. Contagious yawning: The role of self-awareness and mental state attribution. Cogn Brain Res 2003;17:223–227

impaired in subjects suffering from empathy disorders, such as autism:
- Senju A, Maeda M, Kikuchi Y, Hasegawa T, Tojo Y, Osanai H. Absence of contagious yawning in children with autism spectrum disorder. Biology Letters 2007;3:706–708

72% of the dogs yawned after observing a human experimenter yawn:
- Joly-Mascheroni RM, Senju A, Shepherd AJ. Dogs catch human yawn. Biol Let 2008;4:446–448

just the sound of a yawn can elicit a yawning response:
- Arnott SR, Singhal A, Goodale MA. An investigation of auditory contagious yawning. Cogn Affect Behav Neurosci 2009;9:335–342

yawning in dogs can also indicate mild to moderate stress:
- Beerda B, Schilder MBH, van Hooff JARAM, de Vries HW, Mol JA. Behavioural, saliva cortisol and heart rate responses to different types of stimuli in dogs. Appl Anim Behav Sci 1998;58:365–381

The authors of this study therefore set two goals:
- Romero T, Konno A, Hasegawa T. Familiarity bias and physiological responses in contagious yawning by dogs support link to empathy. PLoS ONE 2013;8(8): e71365

primates other than humans (chimpanzees, bonobos, gelada baboons, and stump-tailed macaques) demonstrate contagious yawning:
- Romero T, Konno A, Hasegawa T. Familiarity bias and physiological responses in contagious yawning by dogs support link to empathy. PLoS ONE 2013;8(8): e71365

Budgies, a small parrot, also experience contagious yawning with other budgies:
- Miller ML, Gallup GC, Vogel AR, Vicario SM, Clark AB. Evidence for contagious behaviors in budgerigars (*Melopsittacus undulatus*): An observational study of yawning and stretching. Behav Process 2012;89:264–270

Chapter 36. Teacher's Pet
Researchers in Hungary undertook a relatively simple, but fascinating, study:
- Kis A, Szakadát S, Gásci M, Kováks M, Simor P, Török C, Gombos F, Bódizs R, Topál J. The interrelated effect of sleep and learning in dogs (*Canis familiaris*); an EEG and behavioural study. Sci Rep 2017;7:41873

Chapter 37. Perfect Practice Doesn't Make Perfect
studying how people learn made an interesting discovery:
- Wymbs NF, Bastian AJ, Celnik PA. Motor skills are strengthened through reconsolidation. Curr Biol 2016;26(3):338-343

Chapter 38. Is Your Dog a Social Butterfly?
difference between dogs and wolves is that dogs have greater behavioral plasticity:
- Frank H. Evolution of canine information processing under conditions of natural and artificial selection. Z Tierpsychol 1980;53:389-399

meaning they may be more socially flexible than previously believed:
- Udell MAR, Dorey NR, Wynne CDL. What did domestication do to dogs? A new account of dogs' sensitivity to human actions. Biol Rev Camb Philos Soc 2010;85:327-345

an area on chromosome 6 that was quite different between dogs and wolves:
- von Holdt BM, Shuldiner E, Koch IJ, Kartzinel RY, Hogan A, Brubaker L, Wanser A, Stahler D, Wynne CDL, Ostrander EA, Sinsheimer JS, Udell MAR. Structural variants in genes associated with human Williams-Beuren syndrome underlie stereotypical hypersociability in domestic dogs. Sci Adv 2017;3:e1700398

Chapter 39. Who is That Dog in the Mirror
the most basic of self-concepts – the ability to recognize that it has a body:
- Gallup FF Jr. Chimpanzees: Self-recognition. Science 1970;167(3914):86-7

a type of "olfactory mirror" test:
- Horowitz A. Smelling themselves: Dogs investigate their own odours longer when modified in an "olfactory mirror" test. Behav Process 2017;148:16-19

suggesting that they have no concept of themselves as a physical being:
- Brownell CA, Serwas S, Ramani GB. "So big": The development of body self-awareness in toddlers. Child Dev 2007;78:1426-1440

this test was adapted to dogs:
- Lenkei R, Faragó T, Zsilák B, Pongràcz P. Dogs (*Canis familiaris*) recognize their own body as a physical obstacle. Nature Port Sci Rep 2021;11:2761

Chapter 40. Can We Talk About the Ideal Family Dog?
A detailed, accessible discussion of canine structure and how it affects function has been published:
- Zink C, Schlehr M. Working dog structure: Evaluation and relationship to function. Front Vet Sci 2020;7:559055

Index

A
adenosine tri-phosphate (ATP), 46
advanced glycation end-products (AGEs), 80, 81
Adventure Walks, 23
aerobic, 2, 5, 23
age, 56, 59, 73, 76-78, 104
aggression, 100, 109, 129, 130
agility, 7, 11, 18, 10, 28, 29, 30, 48, 51, 52, 53, 55, 57, 58, 66, 69, 90, 117, 120, 122, 132
alarming stimulus, 109
Amino acids, 85
Antioxidants, 73, 85, 86, 90
anxiety, 100, 130
arthritis, 12, 25, 27, 34, 38, 51, 52, 74, 78, 81, 83, 85, 90, 91
articular facets, 8, 135
assess, 3, 6, 7, 11, 111
assistance dog work, 7

B
Back pain/injuries, 12
Balance, 5, 10, 14, 36
balanced exercise program, 5
barn hunt, 7
Basenji, 124
Beg, 8, 9, 13, 33
Behavioral health, 129
Bernese Mountain Dog, 74, 124
biceps tendinopathy, 12
Body condition, 44, 74, 76-78
body condition scoring, 74
Border Collie, 29, 55
Boxer, 124

C
canned food, 81, 82, 85, 141
cardiopulmonary, 5, 28
carpal arthritis, 51, 52
Carpal Injuries, 57
chemical messenger, 39
chromosome 123-125
clinical trials, 32, 47
cognitive, 69, 70, 81, 86, 104, 127
Cognitive Bias, 100-102
Contagious Yawning, 115
core, 4, 6-15, 26, 33, 34, 38, 67
COVID-19, 87, 129

cranial cruciate ligament (CCL) 12, 38
curcumin, 90-92, 142

D
dewclaws, 51-53, 55, 56, 138
Diagonal Leg Lifts, 6, 14
digit, 53-56
digit injuries, 55
Discomfort Index, 43
Drug, 39, 91, 103, 104
dynamic, 16 - 18

E
ear infections, 88
easy tricks, 66
Emotions, 109, 110
endurance, 28, 29, 34, 70
Environment, 104
Evaluate Fitness, 3
eyebrow, 112, 113, 114
Eyes, 112

F
fast CAT, 7, 29
fear, 100, 109, 127, 130
field trials, 7, 22, 36, 51, 103
flexibility, 2, 5, 14, 36
flyball, 7, 28, 29, 131
Food tracking, 132
force, 7, 11
forelimb, 51, 52, 53
front limb, 11, 12, 18, 67, 94
Front Limb Injuries, 67

G
genes, 69, 70, 90, 91, 123, 125
Genetics, 43, 69, 70
geriatric, 7, 13, 14, 25, 27
Golden Paste, 91, 92
Golden Retriever, 37, 59, 78, 131
Good for the Soul, 5, 68, 119
Great Pyrenees, 124
gut microflora, 89

H
hamstrings, 4, 6
Harness, 8, 94-97, 132
Hearing, 110
heat, 41, 43, 45, 80, 82, 92, 104, 107, 108, 132
Heat Susceptibility, 44
herding, 7, 36, 52, , 53, 72
Hide and seek, 133
hierarchy of evidence, 32, 47
Hopkins, 120, 121, 122
hunt tests, 7, 22, 29, 103, 131

I
iliopsoas, 8, 12, 38, 40, 50, 60
Iliopsoas injuries, 12
Inflammatory Food, 79
infraspinatus, 3
IGP, 7, 22, 29
Irish Wolfhound, 71, 130

J
Jack Russell Terrier, 124
Joint-Protective Nutraceuticals, 85
joule, 47

K
Kibble, 65, 79-83, 86, 89
Kong™, 64, 118

L
ladder, 14, 23, 33
Ladder Work, 23
LAOM, 112-114
laser, 46-50
lateral abdominal muscles, 4, 12
LED light, 47
levator anguli occuli medialis, 112
Light Therapy, 46
longevity, 2, 7, 25, 73, 76, 78, 80, 81, 83, 84, 129
low impact, 34
lure, 7, 10, 18, 122
lure coursing, 7

M
Maillard reaction, 80
Malassezia, 87, 88

medial shoulder syndrome, 12
Miniature Schnauzer, 124
Mirror, 126, 128
logistic regression analysis, 55

N
non-concussive, 5, 8
nonsteroidal anti-inflammatory drug, 91
nosework, 18, 90, 91, 132
NSAID, 91

O
obedience, 11, 18, 48-50, 92, 111, 120
obese, 37, 44, 76, 78
Olfaction, 110
olfactory, 103, 104, 126
Omega-3 Fatty Acids, 85
Optimistic, 100
Osteoarthritis, 74, 78, 81, 83, 85, 90, 91
Overheat, 43
overload, 6, 9, 17, 25-27, 31, 32, 34, 40, 41, 67
overweight, 44, 74, 76-78
Oxytocin, 98, 99, 101, 113, 115

P
Pain, 8, 12, 17, 25, 27, 38, 40, 46, 59, 60, 62, 85, 88, 90, 91, 106, 129, 130
Pariah Dog, 124
Paw Preference, 109, 110
PBMT, 46-49
peptide hormone, 98
photobiomodulation therapy, 46
physical activity, 34, 43, 73, 119
Play Ball, 38, 39-42
police/military work, 7
Previcox®, 91
Probiotics, 85
Proprioception, 5, 6, 15, 20-23, 32-36

Pug, 124
puppies, 13, 14, 21, 27, 107, 108
Puzzle Games, 64

Q
quads, 4, 6

R

rally, 7, 29, 122
RAOL, 112, 113, 114
rear limb, 11, 16, 51, 67
Rear limb injuries, 67
Reducing Injuries, 32
rehabilitation, 12, 38, 50, 51, 66, 68, 120
Reps and Sets, 25
resistance, 5
retractor anguli occuli lateralis, 112
retrieving, 11, 28-31
Rocket Dog, 14, 15
Roll Over, 14

S

Scent Games, 65
Scents, 103
Scent work, 7
scientific evidence, 8, 16, 24, 46, 84
search and rescue, 7
self-image, 126
senior, 7, 13, 14, 25, 132, 133
Sensory Lateralization, 109
shoulder, 3
Shoulder injuries, 12
Sit Up, 9
Sit-Stand-Sit, 14
Social Behavior, 123
speed, 7, 12, 17, 22, 25, 30, 36, 57, 65, 70, 90, 101, 102, 122
stacked position, 3
stage of life, 7
Stamina, 28-31
Stand-Down-Stand, 14
static, 16-18
strength, 2, 5-9, 11, 13, 14, 15, 17, 18, 23, 25-34, 42, 46, 68, 90, 103, 111
stretch, 9, 12, 16, 17, 30
Structure, 12, 38, 44, 57, 80, 90, 98, 129, 130
Subclinical or Chronic Diseases, 105
Superpower, 106
supplements, 84-86, 141
supraspinatus, 3
Supraspinatus tendinopathy, 12
systematic review, 32, 33, 47

T

tear staining, 89
telomere, 71-73
Temperament, 129
tendinopathy, 12

The Crawl, 15
Tissue Tent Test, 75
Train Some Tricks, 65
Training, 2, 9, 11, 93, 117, 122
triceps, 3

U

Usain Bolt, 16, 29

V

ventral abdominal muscles, 4, 8, 14
Village Dogs from Puerto Rico, 124
Vision, 109
voluntary movement, 33

W

Walking a Peanut Ball, 15
walk, 5, 23, 33-37, 68, 94, 97, 118, 132
walking, 14-16, 18, 37, 57, 94, 95
Warm-Up, 18
watt, 47
wavelengths, 47
WBC, 91
weight-to-height ratio, 56
Williams-Beuren Syndrome, 123
wolf, 112-114
Wolves, 124

Y

yawning, 115, 116
yeast, 87-89